Fresh

Fresh

Great Simple Seafood

MITCHELL TONKS

MICHAEL JOSEPH
an imprint of
PENGUIN BOOKS

MICHAEL JOSEPH

Published by the Penguin Group
Penguin Books Ltd, 80 Strand, London WC2R 0RL, England
Penguin Putnam Inc., 375 Hudson Street, New York, New York 10014, USA
Penguin Books Australia Ltd, 250 Camberwell Road, Camberwell, Victoria 3124, Australia
Penguin Books Canada Ltd, 10 Alcorn Avenue, Toronto, Ontario, Canada M4V 3B2
Penguin Books India (P) Ltd, 11 Community Centre,
Panchsheel Park, New Delhi – 110 017, India
Penguin Books (NZ) Ltd, Cnr Rosedale and Airborne Roads,
Albany, Auckland, New Zealand
Penguin Books (South Africa) (Pty) Ltd, 24 Sturdee Avenue,
Rosebank 2196, South Africa

Penguin Books Ltd, Registered Offices: 80 Strand, London WC2R 0RL, England

www.penguin.com

First published 2004
1

Set in 9/11pt Trade Gothic
Designed by Nicky Barneby
Typeset by Rowland Phototypesetting Ltd, Bury St Edmunds, Suffolk
Printed in Great Britain by Clays Ltd, St Ives plc

A CIP catalogue record for this book is available from the British Library

ISBN 0–718–14628–X

To Penny

'The best seafood dishes I have eaten are those
that required the least effort.'

Contents

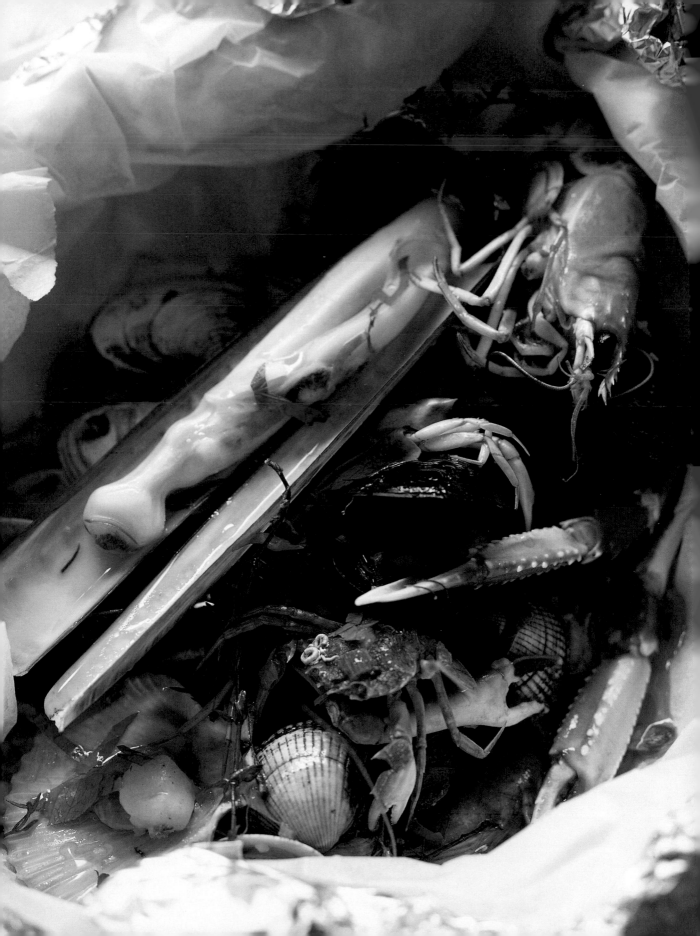

Fish is not only part of my life but also my lifestyle. I eat it regularly at home. It fits in with my life because it's easy, fun to cook, and everyone around me enjoys it. I love the seasonality of seafood; it means there is always something to look forward to. The fishmonger's slab can only reflect the season and the weather: good weather means lots of fish, bad means only a little, it's as simple as that. I have a great sense of excitement when I am going to buy fish: getting to the fishmonger's early to find he has only got two red mullet that day, and buying one of them – it's thrilling. I would love to see more early queues at the fishmonger's, but for many people there is an invisible barrier between themselves and fish cookery – there doesn't seem to be the confidence that they might have with a joint of beef or lamb. I can understand this, because it is where I started out from too.

I became a fishmonger eight years ago when I opened my first shop in Bath. I really wanted to work with fish. Everyone told me I was mad, but I knew that the only madness would be not to do it. My knowledge was limited to that of an enthusiast, but that was enough, and stood me in better stead than most other qualifications I could have had. With no knowledge or experience, I had no fears. All I could do was gain experience, make mistakes, and learn. It was a great time. I bought from, and sold to, some great people. I worked daily with some of the finest produce you can imagine and learnt the most important thing, that good produce is everything.

I also had the pleasure of answering everyday questions about fish and how to cook it. We all need the basics explained and a few pointers to inspire and give us confidence, and this book is based around those questions. It was so rewarding when a customer would shout across the queues in the shop, 'Did the sea bass thing yesterday, brilliant, thanks!'

I have had some funny experiences while learning about fish. In the very early days, for example, I had quite a few kilos of crabs which I had intended to cook for my customers and put in my Saturday window display. Saturday was the busiest day and I liked to lay it on. I put the crabs in the fridge while they were still alive, only to find that by morning they looked dead, all twenty-five of them! Still, I thought, they could be piled into a heap in the window, but not be sold. I wouldn't sell or cook dead shellfish, but at least they would look good. Within a few hours of opening the crowds had gathered, more so than usual. Another great day, I thought, until I looked at the display, which was in a piece of the bow of an old rowing boat called *First Lady*. The crabs were all over the place, they hadn't been dead, just bloody cold! The customers laughed – they thought it was staged. I like to make my windows exciting but dancing crabs is not really my style!

While I was fishmongering I taught myself to cook. I cooked what I liked to eat and was never short of ideas, inspired by the fish and shellfish that would arrive at the shop every day. When I opened the first FishWorks seafood café above the shop I knew how and what I wanted to cook. It was easy. Fish cookery is easy. You keep it simple, it's the best way.

It starts with the produce, being able to buy confidently and knowing what's what. Recognizing fresh fish is no harder than picking out good fruit and vegetables, and with a bit of experience the signs of a sea-fresh fish will become obvious. I could describe what to look for – the clear eyes, the bright gills, the shine and firmness of the flesh – but unless you've actually seen what I mean there may still be some doubt in your mind. I want you to be able to buy with confidence. On page 7 I have put together a buying guide with photographs showing what I look for when I am buying fish to cook at home, or at the coastal markets for our restaurants and fishmongers' counters. You will soon be able to recognize what to buy and what not to. I've given a few other tips too, for example, dressing a crab is not hard: take out the inedible bits and take a hammer and pick to the rest. The photographs will show you which those inedible bits are. I don't think you need to know how to fillet or gut fish, unless you are going to catch your own, so I haven't included this. It's a job for your fishmonger – that's what he's there for and if you ask him he will appreciate his skills being put to good use. He probably has a family recipe or two passed down from a fisherman he knows, and they could turn out to be the best you've come across.

Good fresh ingredients will shout for themselves and a good fish supper is a celebration. A whole fish simply roasted with wild oregano, a sprinkle of sea salt and a glug of good olive oil is a *great* occasion to share and enjoy.

My recipes are about fresh ingredients, prepared and put together simply. My food has to fit into my life, which I am sure is similar to most people's. We have a frantic breakfast time during the week getting everyone off to school, and a lazier one on Sunday. Poached eggs and smoked haddock fit the weekends perfectly but not the week. The kids bring their friends back at weekends and I never know how many there'll be, so cooking for six or more is regular for me. It has to be quick and easy because I like to join in with everyone else's life too.

Some things are obvious starters, like mussels and smoked salmon, but turbot and bass sound as if they should be a main course. The general rule is a smaller amount to start and a bigger amount to serve as main, but quite often one of my side dishes and some bread on the table before the food arrives means that when dining family-style one course will do.

Each recipe has a note that tells you what to ask the fishmonger for, and if possible a few alternatives. And in many of the recipes I've given a note on serving, to help you get the best out of bringing a dish to the table. Seafood doesn't have to have fancy garnishes, and heavy sauces do nothing but disguise it; good fish speaks for itself, it doesn't need anything else. Sometimes, however, I've suggested a side dish to go with it. Many of the recipes have a 'Try this too' suggestion: for example, a handful of chilli can change everything! Think of my recipes as a source of inspiration, not a rigid set of rules. Be flexible, have some fun and enjoy!

If you need any more convincing, visit some of the restaurants and markets I have suggested in the final section of the book. They are fabulous, a real treat and a great experience: I will never forget my first visits to Newlyn, the Paris market of Rungis or the Boqueria in Barcelona. I love the hustle and bustle, the characters, the sound of the auctioneer, and all that great fish. FishWorks is all about this type of experience too; it is based on it – busy fishmongers with tables, open early until late, selling and cooking fish from when the first fishmonger gets in until the last chef goes home. People look, chat, ask advice and eat and drink all in the same place, creating so much atmosphere and excitement – it's fantastic.

I want you to feel that you can cook all the recipes in this book and be confident they will turn out just like the pictures. You can rely on the recipes, I know your next meal may depend on one of them!

Fish and Shellfish: A Really Helpful Buying Guide

Learning how to choose the best fish is probably the most valuable thing I can share with you. Great food is not about fancy technique and complicated cooking. Shop well and relax about the cooking, it's more fun. Start with the best produce you can find, and you will give yourself a wonderful opportunity to keep it simple and show it off.

The freshness of the fish you buy can be affected by so many things, the main one being the weather. In bad weather boats can't go to sea and catch fish. What is landed becomes expensive, and merchants will hang on to and sell anything they can to keep their customers supplied with fish and get them over a period of poor fishing. Fish doesn't keep for long in warm summer temperatures either, even on a boat or market floor. It is a fresh, wild, totally organic, hunted food, and that means it is perishable.

Fish should be stored on ice at zero degrees; the ice melts and takes any bacteria away with the meltwater. Under these conditions it can be stored for more than a week after being caught and still be in good condition, but for every degree the temperature rises above zero the quality gets worse. An hour too long on a deck or market floor in summer can be damaging and costly. Everybody in the supply chain must treat the fish with care, and it goes through a few changes of hands before it gets to the shops: from the fisherman, to the market for auction, then to the fish merchant for processing and distribution, and lastly to the retailer, and between them all is specialist packing and transport. What always amazes me is that the people involved can be at opposite ends of the country, or the other side of the world from each other. It is a twenty-four-hour business, and while we sleep fresh supplies of fish are driven and flown all over the place to get to us. It makes us appreciate a good fish counter. With all this going on, though, a lot depends on all these guys in the middle. 'Fresh in this morning' doesn't mean caught yesterday.

You are the one with the final say; you decide what to buy. Good fish is worth travelling for, either to the coast or to a fishmonger with a reputation. He will appreciate you going to him, and you can't help but enjoy the surprises that the ever-changing counter will sparkle with when you get there.

But how do you pick out what's good?

The photographs on pages 10–11 show what I look for when I am buying fish. They will teach you how to recognize a good buy. You can see not only what really good fish looks like, but what the poor stuff looks like too. It is just as important to be able to recognize quickly what you don't want. Somewhere between the two will be your decision to buy. Think about it as a sliding scale: try to buy fish that looks like the sparkling fresh pictures – the more it looks like the 'tired' ones, the more you will be losing out. Remember, fresh fish doesn't have a 'fish' smell and neither should your fishmonger's shop. Old fish starts to smell as nature breaks it down. When you get your fish home, store it in the fridge, loosely covered with a damp cloth, and eat it within forty-eight hours to enjoy it at its best. Domestic refrigerators don't run at zero and you may not have the luxury of crushed ice unless you have asked the fishmonger for some of his.

When it comes to shellfish such as crab and lobster, it is always best to buy them live, even if you then get the fishmonger to cook them for you. With mussels and clams and other bivalves, ensure they are tightly closed when you buy them; they sometimes open up on a counter or in the fridge because of the cold, but

give them a tap and they should close. If they don't they're for the bin. When you cook them they should easily pop open; if they don't, they're for the bin as well. One thing you must never do is put them in tap water for any length of time, as you will kill them. They are used to living in salt water. A light washing under a running tap to remove all the surface grit and mud is enough. Before the fishmonger gets them they will have lived in salt water tanks for a few days to clear them of any grit and nasties. If the fishmonger has some seaweed, ask him for a handful because it is good for covering shellfish in the fridge. If he doesn't have any, use a few sheets of damp newspaper or a wet cloth. Don't store shellfish for longer than forty-eight hours. Lobsters and crabs are best cooked as soon as you get them home.

Shopping for food is great fun and getting the stuff in is all part of it. When I'm in Spain I love to go to the food markets, like the Boqueria on the Ramblas, in Barcelona. As you walk through the lively bustle of the stalls you'll find the odd bar, next to the greengrocer, in between the butcher and fishmonger, it's great. You can just sit there and take in everything that is going on around you. I long for there to be more markets like that here, but even without the Boqueria I still love Saturdays when I can get up early and go and get the weekend's supplies. There's time to chat, go to the baker, the butcher, the greengrocer, maybe sneak in a brandy or two and enjoy coming home with all the goodies. The way you shop does make a difference.

Bright clear eyes are a first sure sign of freshness

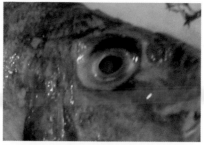

Dull sunken eyes mean a few days the wrong side of fresh

Flesh should be nice and firm: your finger should leave no indentation

Really fresh fish is as stiff as a board: you can hold it from the head or tail – fish-mongers call it 'stiff alive'

Look for a healthy coating of fresh-smelling slime – these dover soles are magnificent

The perfect red mullet, caught by an in-shore boat – all scales on, bright and with golden stripe and white belly. Mullet caught by heavy fishing methods lose their scales, bruise and appear dull pink

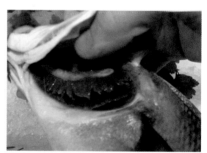

After the eyes look at the gills, they should be deep red in colour – the smell should be nothing more than a fantastic whiff of the sea

This is perfect tuna – a deep translucent red, it just looks great

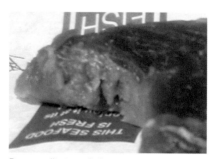

Poor quality tuna is brown or grey with a pearlescent tinge

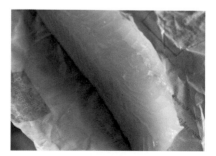

Fish fillets should be firm and opaque – there should be no signs of yellowing

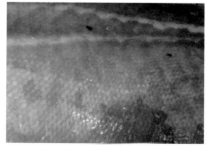

Look at the skin on fish fillets: it should be bright. Unscrupulous fishmongers some-times fillet old fish because the eyes and gills give away too much – best to buy your fish whole and have your fishmonger fillet it for you. This piece of cod is still vibrant and golden on the skin side

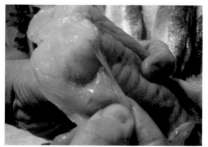

Get the fishmonger to skin your monkfish and take away the pink membrane underneath

Skate wings have a pink tinge – older ones go grey

Fresh fish shines: it looks like it has just come from the sea

Shellfish should look lively

Sea Tigers

Carabineros

Try all sorts of prawns – frozen at sea is fine as long as they are wild. Farmed are more readily available but the flavour is dull and the texture tough

Avoid scallops if they are sitting in water, as they're sponges and will soak it all up. Ask for dry scallop meat. They should be firm to touch with a sweet smell

Buy live shellfish where you can and cook them yourself – plenty of water and a few handfuls of salt. If you're near the sea then seawater is best of all

Clams and mussels should be tightly closed. Give open ones a tap: if they close they're fine, if not don't buy them – be selective

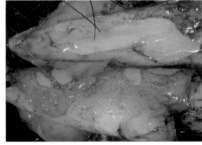

Squid should be pure white with no signs of any pinkness

Buying a cooked crab: turn it over and pull back the flap, you should smell a fresh waft of the sea – nothing stronger. If it's white meat you like then the cock crab has more, while the hen has more rich brown meat and orange coral inside the top shell – great for pasta dishes

Cooked lobsters should feel heavy for their size. Stretch out the tail: it should spring back and curl underneath; if it just hangs limp it's a few days old

Simple Everyday Tips for Cooking and Preparing Fish

When I say fish cookery is easy, I really mean it.

The scaling, the gutting, all the messy jobs, are done by your fishmonger, so you don't have to worry about anything but the cooking. If you are buying squid, get him to clean it for you, and if you want the ink, buy it in a sachet, it's cleaner. If you cook your own crab you will enjoy it at its very best, but you can still get your fishmonger to do it for you if you like (we have to cook and dress at least fifteen or twenty crabs on a busy Saturday). You just need to know what to take out and what to eat, that's all. There is no mystery to it and nothing inside the crab will harm you. The brown meat inside the top shell can look a little off-putting at first, and often it doesn't look how you might expect. Scrape it *all* out, mash it with a fork and it will look a little more like the brown crabmeat that you may be familiar with. Have a look at the following page and you will see what I mean.

Fish is forgiving. It doesn't go from under-cooked to over-cooked while you blink. It will wait in a warm place for a few minutes while you finish your sauce or vegetables; being neglected under the grill is what it doesn't like. Fish such as cod, with soft large flakes, is better roasted or baked. The less you handle it the better: it can break up if you play around with it too much. Firmer fish like monkfish, tuna, gurnard and turbot are more robust and stand up to a bit of handling and a fierce grilling.

I always use the oven when I am cooking fish. I may start it in a pan, under the grill, or even on the barbecue, but I always finish it in the oven, unless the fish are small, like sardines. Think about the heat of a grill: it's direct and from the top. So you will only cook the top of the fish and, while you wait for the bottom to cook, the top will overcook. If you try to turn it over you may break it. Try this next time. Get the grill hot first. Put the fish on a tray so it can be placed under the grill and then removed, and grill for 5–6 minutes until the skin is crisp on the side you will serve uppermost. If you are cooking a piece of fillet or if it is skinless, like skate, rub it with some butter to help colour it – you want it to look appetizing. Then put it straight into a preheated oven set to its maximum temperature. The fish will cook evenly in the all-round heat, keeping it moist. Check it regularly; you will soon get used to your own oven and get the timings right. As a rough guide for fish like bass and bream weighing around 450 g, 5–6 minutes under the grill then 15–20 minutes in the oven is perfect every time. Roast a mixture of mussels, clams, cockles and prawns with a dozen or so garlic cloves, a splash of wine and some parsley and you will realize just how useful it can be.

Chunks or fillets of cod, haddock, turbot or brill can be browned in a pan first. Heat some vegetable or groundnut oil until really hot (cool oil will cause the fish to stick) – save your olive oil for drizzling over the fish when it is cooked. Put the fish in the pan, cook for 4–5 minutes, then turn it with a pair of tongs. When it is nicely coloured, put the whole pan in the oven or transfer the fish to a roasting tray, and let the oven do the rest. Check the fish regularly until it is firm and moist. You will soon get used to using this method and get perfectly cooked fish every time.

Mussels, clams, cockles and other bivalves, as they are called, are all prepared in much the same way. If you can cook mussels, then you can cook any type of clam. They must be closed before you cook them and open when they are cooked. You can steam them in a drop of wine or water, roast them in the oven or boil them in a soup – they are really easy-going, like most shellfish.

On the next two pages are notes and photographs of what I think are the most useful everyday tips; they are not complicated and need little explanation.

Picking cooked crab

Turn the cooked crab on its back, open it with your thumbs and take off the top shell

The feathery things are dead men's fingers – they're harmless

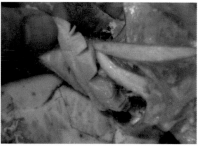

Give them a tug, they come off easily

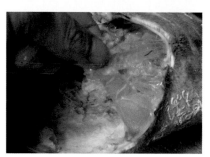

Pull away all the bits of membrane

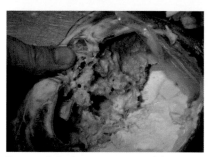

Scrape all the brown meat out of the top shell – mash it up. It's all edible but might not look like it at first.

Smash and crack the legs, claws and body and pick out all the white meat – the body contains the sweetest meat

Preparing cooked lobster

Insert a heavy knife through the back of the lobster's head. Press down and lever the knife towards the tail

The green meat and red coral is fantastic to eat so don't discard it. Just remove the plastic-looking membrane from behind the eyes and the black vein running through the tail, if there is one

The claws just need a firm crack with a heavy knife to break them open

Split langoustines down the belly before cooking. Like lobster, the meat in the head is great to eat

A crab must be killed before cooking. Insert a screwdriver through the bottom then cook it in plenty of salted water

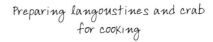

Preparing langoustines and crab for cooking

Mussels and clams

Give the beards on mussels a gentle tug to remove them

Mussels and clams can be simply opened like oysters and eaten with a squeeze of lemon – amazing

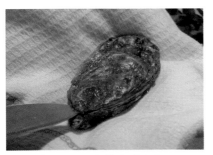

Use a sharp oyster knife (pointed ones are better than rounded) and protect your hand with a folded cloth when opening the oyster. Go in by the hinge or at the side, whichever you find easier. Try not to break any shell into the oyster

The perfect oyster – plump and full of sea-water. A dry shell with no liquid inside will mean the oyster is dead – throw it away

Oysters

Cooking a piece of fish

Start your fish on the top of the stove and always finish it off by putting it in the oven on maximum heat for a few minutes

When a piece of fish is properly cooked a white milky liquid oozes from it. This is full of proteins and means that the fish is moist, juicy and ready to serve. Get to know your oven and you will have perfect fish every time

Basics for the Kitchen

Basics are things that you need and use regularly – like olive oil, butter and salt. My own basics include roasted tomatoes, gooseberry vinegar, wine vinegar, spice pastes, good garlic butter and loads of fresh herbs. It makes your cooking so much more exciting when you've got stuff like this knocking about. It keeps your kitchen alive. Keep your stocks topped up so that you can always grab a chunk of something or use a drizzle of something – it'll go a long way towards making good fish taste great.

Buy yourself some good dry store ingredients: nuts, dried chillies, spices and herbs. If you've got a bunch of basil that's starting to wilt because it's been kept in the wrong place or you haven't got round to using it, make some pesto. It will help you decide what you are going to cook over the next few days. Make fresh tomato sauce in quantity and store it in sterilized jars in the fridge. It's a great way to take advantage of the cheap boxes of over-ripe tomatoes you sometimes find at the greengrocer's. If you get a few spare minutes in the week and you know you are going to need a bit of green curry paste for the weekend, make it then – and while you've got the food processor out, make twice as much as you need. It will become a basic for a few weeks after that.

The recipes and notes in this section are important and will make your life easier. Stock up with some good olive oil – you'll need lots of it. By good olive oil I mean cheaper extra virgin. By best olive oil I mean estate-bottled first cold pressing. Try out different oils – a drizzle of your favourite, and some sea salt, will be all you need on a piece of roasted fish. But you can let a good piece of fish down if you don't buy your other ingredients well. Put as much energy into shopping for vegetables, salad and extras like olive oil as you would for your fresh fish.

Basics for me aren't boring things like stocks, they are things I can use with any-thing, not just fish. What am I going to do with a pint of fish stock if I suddenly decide to eat a fresh ball of mozzarella for supper? You don't have that problem with a jar of roasted tomatoes and a few tablespoons of pesto. Keep your kitchen alive and full of possibility.

Tempura Batter

This is the batter I always use. When it's cooked it's crisp, light and firm. Sometimes the addition of a splash of beer can make a difference if you are using it for frying fish like cod, haddock or plaice.

You will need 4 tablespoons plain flour — 4 tablespoons cornflour — salt and freshly ground black pepper — 1 small bottle of sparkling mineral water straight from the fridge

To make Mix the flours together and add salt and freshly ground black pepper. Gradually whisk in enough of the water to give you a double cream consistency. Dip your fish straight into this mixture and deep fry.

Basic Beurre Blanc

This is a really versatile classic sauce to serve with fish. When you've mastered the basic sauce you can add all sorts of flavours, such as almonds, rosemary, a few salted capers, citrus juices, herbs – just about anything really. My favourite is beurre blanc with a few sea-urchin roes stirred in at the last minute.

You will need (makes enough for 2 servings) 3 shallots, very finely chopped — 50 ml white wine — 50 ml white wine vinegar — 50 ml double cream — 50 g butter

To make Put the shallots, wine and vinegar in a saucepan and boil until only a teaspoonful of the liquid is left. Add the cream and reduce again by half. Remove from the heat and gradually whisk in the butter, then add any other flavours you fancy. Be creative – have a bit of fun.

Sea Urchin Beurre Blanc

If you have never eaten sea urchins then you must try them. The parts you eat are the small orange fingers contained inside. The flavour is like iodine and mouthfuls of sea. Sea urchins are fantastic stirred into scrambled eggs, great mixed with butter and tossed with linguine or spaghettini, or dropped into the top of a runny freshly boiled egg then fished out with a thin buttered finger of hot toast (caviar is good eaten like that too – you must try it, it spices up Sunday breakfast in bed!).

You will need (makes enough for 2 servings) basic beurre blanc (see page 18) — 1 good teaspoon fresh sea-urchin roe

To make Mix the beurre blanc and roe together and spoon on top of grilled fish such as turbot, flaky cod, raw oysters, grilled or raw clams and fat, juicy scallops.

Béchamel or White Sauce

This is the only recipe I use for this basic white sauce. It has never let me down.

You will need (makes 300 ml – enough for 4 as a sauce) ½ an onion — 2 bay leaves — 4 cloves — 200 ml milk — 100 ml double cream — 8 peppercorns — a pinch of salt — 50 g butter — 1 tablespoon plain flour

To make Make 2 cuts in the onion and stick the bay leaves into them. Push the cloves into the onion, put it into a small pan, and pour in the milk and cream. Add the peppercorns and the salt, then bring to the boil and simmer gently for 5 minutes. Remove from the heat and allow the flavours to infuse for 20 minutes. Remove the onion and peppercorns and pour the infused milk and cream into a jug. Melt the butter gently in a saucepan, then, while the pan is off the heat, sprinkle in the flour a little at a time, stirring until you have a smooth paste. Gradually pour in the milk while gently whisking – don't pour too fast, otherwise you will get lumps. Half-way through pouring, place the pan on the heat and keep whisking and adding milk until the mix-ture has the consistency of double cream. The sauce can be stored in the fridge for a few days and it is worth knocking some up when you have a spare few minutes so that it is there when you need it.

Rich Tomato Sauce for Fish and Pasta

When I travel I love the excitement and the anticipation of what I am going to eat. During my memorable though swift visit to Venice last year my man at the Hotel Umberto recommended a restaurant where his mother ate, Hostaria da Franz. Franz himself greeted us as we stepped off the boat and we spent the after-noon eating at the restaurant and chatting to him. He told us about local ingredients such as the tiny tender little artichokes which are gathered on the small island of St Erasmo between 15 April and 31 June – Franz was very specific about the dates. This is the time when they are at their best. I just loved everything he had to tell us after that.

Tomato sauces are prominent in Italian cookery and should be of a rich, thick consistency, not thin and watery. Franz gave me his recipe, which has evolved in his kitchen over the fourteen years he has been running his restaurant.

You will need (makes enough for 6 servings) 100 ml good olive oil — salt — ½ an onion, chopped — 1 clove of garlic, crushed — 1 small stick of celery, chopped — 1 small carrot, peeled and chopped — a pinch of paprika — a pinch of chilli powder — a sprig of fresh thyme — a pinch of sugar — a splash of white wine — 500 g ripe tomatoes, roughly chopped – use the very best you can get (if you feel the tomatoes need an extra something add a squeeze of good Italian double-concentrated tomato purée)

To make Put the oil and a pinch of salt into a heavy-based pan. Add the onion, garlic, celery and carrot and cook gently without frying or browning for 10–12 minutes until softened. Then add the paprika, chilli powder, thyme and just a little pinch of sugar. Add a splash of white wine and then the tomatoes to the pan and continue to simmer gently until the tomatoes have completely melted. Never cover the pan, otherwise the sauce will become watery. Leave the pan uncovered, and the sauce will thicken as it reduces. You can leave it as it is and have a chunky, rustic sauce and I often do this; however, I sometimes put it all through my vegetable mouli and squeeze out every last bit of flavour, making it luxuriously smooth. If you find at this stage that the sauce is a little watery, simply put it back in the pan and reduce it until you have a creamier consistency. But this should not be necessary.

Try this too . . . This is a great way to take advantage of a good home-grown crop. To make a roasted tomato sauce, see the instructions for oven-roasted tomatoes on page 44, add a touch of chilli, and follow the rest of the recipe above. Finish with torn fresh basil before serving.

Pesto

Freshly made pesto is one of the most versatile ingredients there is. It can be tossed into pasta, spooned into sauces, stirred into soups, butter or seafood stews – the possibilities are endless. It tastes great and is full of sunny flavours. Home-made pesto is so much better than anything you can buy, so make it in quantity. It will keep for weeks in a jar with a layer of oil on top, stored in the fridge.

You will need (makes enough for 6 servings) a large bunch of fresh basil, stalks removed — 1 clove of garlic — 1 tablespoon pine nuts — 25 g parmesan or pecorino cheese shavings — sea salt to taste — 200 ml good olive oil

To make Put all the ingredients except the olive oil into a food processor and pulse until you have a chunky paste. Gradually, while still pulsing, add the olive oil. If you think it needs more oil, simply put more in, and if you think it is wet enough stop adding it. Easy.

Try this too ... Try the following variations, which are all made and used in exactly the same way as the classic recipe. Change the ingredients but follow the method above. Balance the quantity of the ingredients in each one to suit your own taste. Where I have used chilli, add more or less depending on how hot you like it. If using coriander do the same, but add enough olive oil to get the consistency right. The nuts will make the pesto creamy. Each variation makes enough for 6 servings.

Sweet Roasted Pepper, Chilli and Coriander Pesto

You will need 1 red roasted pepper, peeled and de-seeded — 1 clove of garlic — 1 tablespoon pine nuts — a large handful of fresh coriander leaves — 25 g pecorino cheese — 200 ml olive oil

Try this with tuna or freshly steamed mussels.

Thai Basil, Coconut and Lime Pesto

You will need a large handful of Thai or holy basil leaves (this recipe doesn't work with Mediterranean basil) — 1 clove of garlic — a 5 cm piece of fresh root ginger, roughly chopped — 1 tablespoon peeled macadamia or candle nuts — 1 small fresh green chilli — lime juice — a dash of Thai fish sauce — 200 ml coconut milk

Great for drizzling over red snapper, mahi-mahi, and other exotic species which have been cooked over a barbecue.

Parsley, Mint, Walnut and Feta Pesto

You will need a small handful of walnuts — a small handful of fresh parsley — a small handful of fresh mint — 1 clove of garlic — 100 g crumbled feta or halloumi cheese — lemon juice to taste — sea salt

Great on red mullet or roasted bream.

Parsley, Garlic, Hazelnut and Salted Anchovy Pesto

You will need a small bunch of fresh parsley — 1 clove of garlic — 1 tablespoon hazelnuts — 6 salted anchovy fillets — 25 g parmesan or pecorino cheese — 100–150 ml olive oil — sea salt

This is ace on freshly grilled scallops or sardines.

Using the same method and different ingredients, you can create other sauces with that wonderful freshness and immediacy. They will all capture the essence of the ingredients and go so well with an already brilliant simply grilled piece of fresh fish. They can also transform simple vegetables to create a whole new array of side dishes. Try new season's asparagus with traditional pesto or with the parsley, mint, walnut and feta; freshly dug potatoes with the parsley, garlic, hazelnut and anchovy; or chargrilled fennel with the sweet pepper, chilli and coriander . . .

Mayonnaise

Good home-made mayonnaise can't be beaten, although I always have a jar of shop-bought stuff lurking in the fridge somewhere. It is the base for so many other sauces, tartare sauce for instance. Try flavouring it with fresh chopped mint and capers, or anchovies and fresh parsley. Add a bit of garlic, leave it in the fridge for a few days, then serve it instead of butter or olive oil to spread on fresh, crusty bread before the main meal arrives.

You will need (makes enough for 4 servings) 2 egg yolks — 1 teaspoon Dijon mustard — 1 tablespoon white wine vinegar — 200 ml plain oil, such as groundnut or vegetable — 50 ml olive oil — salt and freshly ground black pepper — optional: juice of $\frac{1}{2}$ a lemon

To make Put the egg yolks into a bowl with the mustard and vinegar and whisk. Put the bowl on top of a folded tea-towel to stop it slipping, and while whisking pour in the plain oil slowly in a gentle stream. The ingredients should thicken and emulsify together. Lastly add the olive oil until you have a light, pale, creamy mayonnaise. If it needs more oil, use the plain variety. If all the oil has been added and all you've got is liquid then I'm afraid it has split. You can try to rescue it by slowing pouring it on to a few more egg yolks but you will end up with lots more mayonnaise than you need. Lastly season with salt and freshly ground black pepper and add the lemon juice.

Tartare Sauce

You can't beat freshly fried scampi or fish fingers dipped into a good tartare sauce. Fish and chips and fish-cakes just wouldn't be the same without it. The stuff you get in little packs with a pub meal isn't tartare sauce, it just says that on the packet. A good tartare sauce should be what it says: tart, full of pickles, capers and herbs, and have you looking for more when your first helping is gone.

You will need (makes enough for 2 or 3 servings) 1 recipe quantity of mayonnaise (see above) — 1 tablespoon salted capers, rinsed — 6 cornichons, chopped — 1 shallot, finely chopped — 1 tablespoon finely chopped fresh tarragon — sea salt — juice of 1 lemon

To make Put the mayonnaise into a bowl and stir in the other ingredients, adjusting the salt and lemon juice to your taste. It should be quite chunky and if, as I do, you love capers and cornichons, you can add a few more.

Seafood Cocktail Sauce

There is nothing wrong with a good prawn or crab cocktail as long as the prawns are fresh and the crab just boiled and picked, and with a spoonful of this sauce and some crisp lettuce you'll have a great dish.

You will need (makes enough for 2 or 3 servings) 200 ml fresh mayonnaise (see page 23) — 2 tablespoons tomato ketchup — a splash of whisky or brandy — a few drops of Tabasco — a few drops of Worcestershire Sauce — a squeeze of lemon — a pinch of cayenne pepper

To make Simply mix together all the ingredients except the cayenne pepper and taste. You will know the flavour you want: just add tomato ketchup for sweetness, Tabasco for heat and whisky for a kick until it is to your liking. Dress your crab, prawns or anything else, and sprinkle the cayenne over the top.

All-i-oli

The true Catalonian all-i-oli isn't made with eggs – it is just a straight interpretation of the title, which means garlic and oil. The Catalans make an emulsion from pounded juicy garlic cloves and good fruity olive oil. The purist wouldn't even add vinegar or lemon juice, but I think they can be added for a little acidity if you wish. All-i-oli is more pungent than the mayonnaise-style French version. I make it regularly and use it for spreading on bread, for adding to soup and stews, for dunking raw vegetables into and for keeping everyone away from me! It is absolutely delicious spread over a bit of meat before grilling or barbecuing, and even more delicious rubbed over prawns or whole fish.

When all-i-oli is made with good oil its colour is a deep rich yellow, and when you eat it the raw garlic has a peppery kick which lingers in your mouth a long time. It takes 2 minutes to knock together.

You will need (makes 200 ml) 4–5 juicy cloves of garlic, peeled — a good pinch of sea salt — 200 ml ordinary olive oil

To make Roughly chop the garlic, discarding any green shoots that may be lurking in the middle, which can be bitter. Put the garlic into a large pestle and mortar with the salt and grind with a steady circular motion, moving the same way all the time, until you have a thick sticky paste. There should be no lumps at all. Keep grinding, and drizzle in the olive oil a little at a time as if making mayonnaise. The garlic and oil will emulsify. You can add vinegar or lemon juice if you wish, but I don't – I love it the way it is. Store it in the fridge in a covered jar. A few anchovies crushed in the mortar with the garlic are interesting too, although not traditional.

Shellfish Dressing

If you are serving a *fruits de mer*, oysters, or any other raw shellfish, this is a great dressing which you can throw together in a minute. It is also good spooned over freshly grilled shellfish.

You will need (makes enough for 6 servings) 100 ml red wine vinegar — 100 ml tarragon vinegar — a few splashes of Tabasco — 1 shallot, finely chopped — a small handful of fresh parsley, chopped — a good pinch of salt

To make Mix all the ingredients together and serve.

Chilli Jam

This is great to have in the kitchen. Use it with squid, or add a spoonful when frying prawns to coat them in the delicious hot sweet sauce.

You will need (makes about 400 ml) 5–6 large fresh chillies — 600 g ripe tomatoes — 75 g fresh root ginger, peeled and chopped — 50 ml Thai fish sauce — 5 cloves of garlic, peeled — 150 ml red wine vinegar — 350 g caster sugar — a handful of fresh coriander, chopped — juice of 1 lime

To make Put the chillies, whole tomatoes, including the skin and seeds, ginger, fish sauce and garlic into a blender or food processor and blend to a purée. Put the vinegar and sugar into a saucepan, add the purée from the blender and slowly bring to the boil, stirring frequently and removing any scum that may come to the surface. Cook for 30–40 minutes, stirring frequently until a 'jam' consistency is reached. Taste it – if it needs more sweetness add more sugar, more sourness add more vinegar. Keep tasting until you get the balance right. Before serving add the chopped coriander and the lime juice.

FOR SALE
WHITSTABLE OYSTERS
40p
WHITSTABLE NATIVES
80p
WEST WHELKS

Good Garlic Butter

This is a regular in my kitchen. It has so many uses: it can be melted and poured over fish, or stirred into the juices of steamed clams to give them a velvety richness. It can be stirred into a risotto at the last minute instead of plain butter, or melted and added to a hollandaise sauce. Once you have made it, store it in a plastic tub in the fridge, or wrap it in clingfilm and freeze it. I like my garlic butter to be nearly green with herbs. I hate it when it's just chopped garlic in ordinary melted butter – it needs fresh herbs and a squeeze of lemon.

You will need (makes 450 g) 6 plump cloves of garlic — 2 handfuls of fresh curly parsley, chopped — a handful of fresh tarragon, chopped — a few good pinches of salt — 450 g unsalted butter, softened — a dash of Pernod — a squeeze of lemon juice

To make Blend the garlic, herbs and salt in a food processor or chop them finely by hand. Stir this mixture into the softened butter with the Pernod and lemon juice, making sure you work it well in. When I am cooking with this butter I often add a little more parsley or tarragon and sharpen it up with extra lemon and more salt. If you don't fancy Pernod, use brandy.

Anchovy and Rosemary Butter

This has always been a favourite. It is good for fish, good for vegetables, for spreading on croûtons and hot toast, topped with fried oysters. Sage is a good herb to use if there is no rosemary to hand.

You will need (makes 450 g) ½ a jar of salted anchovy fillets with their oil — 2 cloves of garlic — leaves from 2 sprigs of rosemary — 450 g unsalted butter, softened

To make Put the anchovies, garlic and rosemary leaves into a food processor and blend them until smooth, then stir into the softened butter.

It is good to have some of this in the freezer so you can slice a bit off any time you need it. I like to melt it and add some chopped tomato flesh, some fresh parsley and a squeeze of lemon before serving.

Try this too ... Roast or boil some broccoli and pour some melted anchovy and rosemary butter over it. Fantastic.

Montpellier Butter

This is a classic French preparation and brilliant for just popping on to a grilled piece of fish like skate, putting it back under the grill and letting it melt and crust on the top. It can be used with just about anything, and looks good too.

You will need (makes 300 g) 25 g fresh parsley leaves — 25 g fresh chervil or tarragon — 25 g watercress or spinach — 1 shallot — 2–3 small gherkins — 2 cloves of garlic, peeled — 1 hard-boiled egg — 1 raw egg yolk — 75 ml olive oil — 1 pack (250 g) unsalted butter, softened — salt and freshly ground black pepper

To make Blanch the herbs and the watercress or spinach in hot water for a minute. Refresh under cold water and squeeze thoroughly dry in a tea-towel. Put into a food processor with the shallot, gherkins, garlic and hard-boiled egg and blitz until smooth, then add the raw egg yolk and, with the motor running, drizzle in the olive oil. Lastly add the butter, bit by bit, until all the ingredients are amalgamated and smooth. Season with salt and freshly ground black pepper.

Marinating and Spice Mixes

The golden rule for marinating fish is 'Not for too long'. I would say between 1 and 2 hours is plenty. Fiery North African chermoula is so good rubbed inside and out over a sea bream, marinated for half an hour and then grilled over hot coals. Lemon juice, wild oregano, garlic and sea salt brushed over firm fillets of monk-fish an hour before grilling is typical of the Mediterranean.

The simplest marinade of all is lemon juice, salt, garlic and good fruity olive oil, which can be further flavoured with freshly cut sprigs of rosemary. The great thing about all marinated fish dishes is that the marinating time is about the same as the average time it takes to drive to the nearest beach, so you can put the fish in a container with its marinade, sling it in the back of the car with a bag of salad and some bread, and by the time the throw-away barbecue is lit it will just about be ready, saving you the task of spending all day trying to find a place by the sea that serves decent fish!

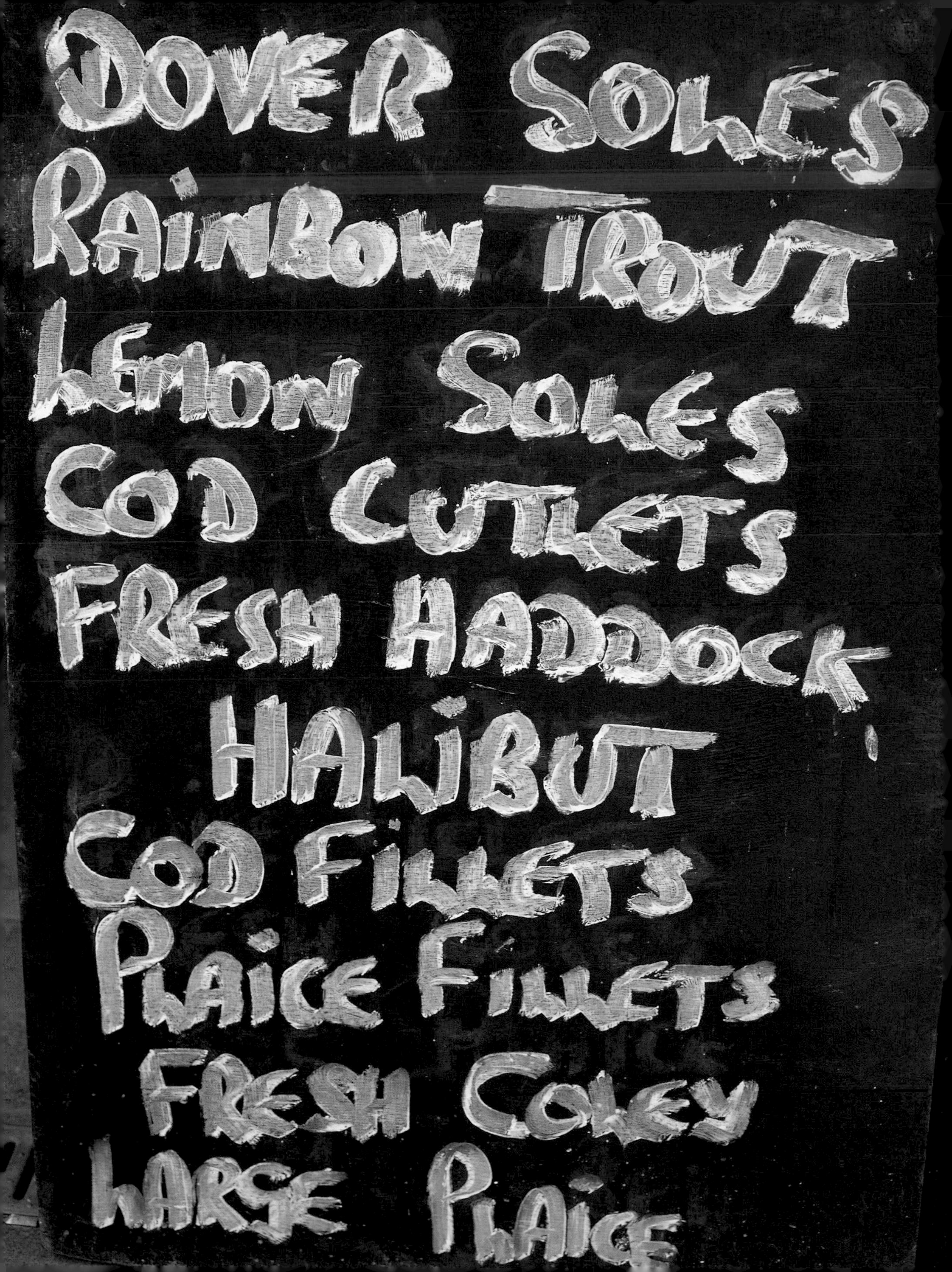

DOVER SOLES

RAINBOW TROUT

LEMON SOLES

COD CUTLETS

FRESH HADDOCK

HALIBUT

COD FILLETS

PLAICE FILLETS

FRESH COLEY

LARGE PLAICE

Chermoula

This is Claudia Roden's recipe, from her brilliant book *Middle Eastern Food*, and is the one I always use. Make this in large quantities – it keeps very well for a week or two in a sealed jar, just covered with a thin layer of oil. I have changed the method slightly and as a variation would suggest the addition of some finely chopped preserved lemon. It's great.

You will need (makes enough for 8-10 servings) 1 tablespoon ground cumin — 1 teaspoon ground coriander — a large bunch of fresh coriander — a large bunch of fresh parsley — a small bunch of fresh mint — 6 large cloves of garlic — 1 tablespoon paprika — a good pinch of cayenne pepper — juice of 2 lemons — 300 ml olive oil

To make For maximum flavour roast and grind the cumin and coriander seeds yourself until you have a fine powder. Pulse the fresh coriander, parsley, mint and garlic in a food processor, then transfer to a bowl and stir in the ground cumin and coriander, paprika, cayenne and lemon juice. Beat in the olive oil.

Salmoriglio

This is a Sicilian marinade which uses flavours that are typical of the Mediterranean. It is wonderful on all sorts of fish, especially sea bream, tuna and swordfish. It can be used as a light marinade or dressing. For best results the fish should be cooked over burning charcoal or wood, but a hot grill plate will do fine.

You will need (makes enough for 2 or 3 servings) 1 teaspoon salt — juice of 1 lemon — 200 ml olive oil — a small handful of fresh oregano leaves, finely chopped — freshly ground black pepper

To make Dissolve the salt in the lemon juice. In a steady stream whisk in the olive oil, then add the herbs and season with freshly ground black pepper. If I am cooking swordfish, tuna or marlin (and this is particularly good with swordfish), I grill it over as high a heat as possible for a few minutes either side, to get that outdoor wood-cooked flavour into the fish, then put it on a plate, prick it several times with a fork and spoon the dressing over, working the back of a spoon over the surface of the fish to ensure the flavours penetrate. Leave it for a few minutes before serving.

Ginger and Lime Marinade

Asian flavours rely totally upon fresh ingredients. When they are fresh and the combination is right the flavours can be stunning. Dried or bottled lemon grass, ginger and coriander just won't do. There are bird's-eye chillies in this marinade and the longer you leave it the hotter it will get, so be careful or you could be in for a surprise. It is particularly good on fish like snapper, king fish and mackerel, or try it with a few prawns which have been split down the back so the marinade gets into them, and then grilled over a fire outdoors. They are delicious.

You will need (makes 250 ml – enough for a good-sized fish) 1 teaspoon sugar — zest and juice of 2 limes — 4 spring onions, white part only — a 5 cm piece of fresh root ginger, peeled — 1–2 bird's-eye chillies – the amount is up to you — 1 tablespoon fresh coriander leaves — a good splash of Thai fish sauce — 150 ml groundnut or vegetable oil

To make Dissolve the sugar in the lime juice. Put the spring onions, ginger, lime zest, chillies and coriander into a food processor and mince until fine. Transfer to a bowl and add the lime juice, fish sauce and vegetable oil. This marinade is best made a few hours in advance or the day before to allow the flavours to develop. Rub it on to your fish before blackening on a grill. It's really fresh and also makes a good dressing or dipping sauce for fresh grilled prawns or freshly boiled crab.

Lemon and Shredded Kaffir Lime Leaf Marinade

This is perfect for shellfish and can be used as a dipping sauce. It's extremely fragrant and is good tossed among cooked noodles to make a salad with dried shrimp and fresh coriander.

You will need (makes enough for marinating a couple of fish) 1 small hot fresh chilli, seeds removed — a pinch of salt — 1 clove of garlic, crushed — juice and pulp of 1 lemon — 3 tablespoons sugar — 3 tablespoons Thai fish sauce — 2–3 kaffir lime leaves, shredded (if you see fresh ones buy them, they freeze very well and are a better option than the jarred variety)

To make In a pestle and mortar pound together the chilli, salt and garlic until you have a smooth paste, then add the pulp and juice of the lemon and the sugar and continue to work together until the sugar has dissolved. Stir in the fish sauce and the shredded lime leaves. If you need more liquid, add cold water, tasting and adjusting the flavours.

ks&CO

vy FILLETS

ETABLE OIL

Indonesian Style Spice Mix

This is a good mix for using with firm fish like snapper and oily ones like king fish, mahi-mahi and mackerel. All these spices are readily available – just make sure they haven't been hanging around too long in the cupboard as they won't have the same pungency and will taste stale. Once made, use this mix within 48 hours to enjoy it at its best.

You will need (makes about 300 ml) 1 tablespoon fennel seeds — 2 tablespoons turmeric — 1 tablespoon cumin seeds — 2½ tablespoons coriander seeds — ½ tablespoon black peppercorns — 1 teaspoon chilli flakes — 1 tablespoon salt — 1 tablespoon sugar — zest and juice of 1 lime — 250 ml coconut milk — a handful of fresh coriander

To make Put the fennel, turmeric, cumin, coriander seeds, peppercorns, chilli flakes and salt into a pan and dry roast until fragrant, then grind to a fine powder either in a spice grinder or a pestle and mortar. Dissolve the sugar in the lime juice, then add it to the coconut milk with the spices, lime zest and fresh coriander. Use as a marinade, or add to a wokful of noodles with some fried squid or prawns.

Seasonings

When we think of seasoning we usually think of salt and pepper. When spices are ground together in different combinations they are great not only as a base for cooking but also for dipping bread, vegetables or cooked food into. I like to play around with ingredients, simply crushing them together in a mortar or putting them in a peppermill in various combinations. You will be really surprised at the results you get. Star anise and fennel seed in the peppermill with black peppercorns and salt can make an interesting combination with a few grilled sardines. Try grinding toasted sesame seed, salt and fresh thyme: sprinkle on to a few scallops before cooking and finish with a squeeze of lemon, or just dip raw vegetables into this mixture.

There are so many spices to choose from: smell them, taste them and let your senses guide you as to which ones will work together. Add vinegar and oil to make a marinade and lemon juice or plain oil to make a spicy dressing. Don't rely just on dried ingredients, always add fresh herbs like coriander, fresh mint or parsley. Fresh mint ground in a mortar with salt and white pepper is wonderful sprinkled over grilled red mullet or tossed into a fresh crab salad. Toast whole spices in a dry pan before you grind them as this will give you the most aromatic flavour.

Gooseberry Vinegar

Making vinegars and pickles is great fun and can really give the store-cupboard a boost. I use vinegars quite a lot, in dressings or stirred into a few fried onions before adding to toppings and stuffings, but this vinegar is so good on its own, especially drizzled over freshly grilled mackerel, or in a dressing for a salad of flaked smoked mackerel and watercress. It is easy to make, won't take much of your time, and once you have mastered the method you can make other flavours such as raspberry, apple and rosemary, chilli and tomato, or strawberry, black pepper and basil. The principles are the same, just replace the gooseberries and sorrel with your chosen alternative.

You will need (makes 1 litre) 1 litre good-quality cider vinegar — 1 kg ripe gooseberries — a good handful of fresh sorrel or baby spinach leaves — grated zest of 1 lemon — salt

To make First boil the vinegar for 3–4 minutes and set aside to cool. Wash the gooseberries and sorrel or spinach and pulse to a chunky paste in a food processor. Stir in the lemon zest and just a pinch of salt, then put into a clean jar, large enough to take the vinegar as well. Pour the vinegar over, cover the jar, and leave to mature for 3–4 weeks, giving it a shake every now and then. Strain through fine muslin and pour into sterilized bottles with tops that can be sealed. Any sediment that may still be in the vinegar will settle in a few days.

Salting your own cod

So why salt cod in the first place? It is an age-old method of preservation which goes back to the eleventh century. The cod is first salted, which removes moisture, then it is dried by the wind, or in specially controlled drying rooms. Before use it needs to be soaked to remove the salt.

Start with a nice fresh piece of cod. Completely cover it with a good coarse rock salt and leave it in the fridge for a few days. The salt will turn to brine and the fish will be firm to touch. Remove the cod from the salt and brush off any excess from the surface. The cod now needs to be soaked in cold water for between 24 and 48 hours, changing the water every 6 hours or so. While soaking it needs to be kept in the fridge. After this time it will be ready to use.

Commercially salted cod definitely needs the full 48 hours soaking. I think the only way to see whether the cod is ready is to cut a tiny bit off the end and taste it. Don't be put off – the raw soaked cod is delicious just thinly sliced and marinated in a bit of lemon juice for 4–5 minutes, then covered with olive oil, chopped garlic and parsley. It makes a wonderful appetizer with drinks. Salt cod is good to have around, it is surprisingly versatile.

Favourite Recipes: Ones You Must Try

It is never just one thing that makes a recipe a favourite – it is a combination of good food, the company and the location. Eating it, sharing it, even talking about it, can fill you with anticipation, excitement and contentment. It's total enjoyment from start to finish. On the island of Burano with Penny and my youngest daughter, Isobel, we ate a couple of small sea bass not half an hour out of the water. They had been filleted then dipped in milk and flour, deep-fried until crisp and served with nothing but a wedge of lemon. It was an easy experience. The fish from the lagoon there is magnificent.

Choosing a favourite is still a challenge, but when you have cooked, eaten and experienced many wonderful dishes the enjoyment and atmosphere created by the best ones make them stand out as brilliant among the rest. Lobster, sea crab and rice stew is simple, delicious and typically Spanish. You can really taste the rich flavours of the shellfish with the garlic, and eating the rice, completely soaked with these flavours, is a comforting experience. Bucatini baked with whole roasted garlic, thyme and shellfish is chewy and full of sweet garlic and cooked shellfish flavour. Bottarga will make you feel like you have eaten a mouthful of the sea, and sautéd spider crab will give you hours of enjoyment, sucking, licking and picking everything from the shell.

The recipes in this section are among my favourites and I would love to think you would try all of them.

Baked Sea Bream, as in the Balearics

My mate big Pete Brown showed me around the island of Menorca a few years ago and introduced me to a fantastic restaurant, S'Espigo, in the port of Mahón. The owners, Anna and Juan, have been doing the cooking and the serving for over seventeen years.

Their food is typically Menorcan. They work with the most wonderful produce: everything in Menorca is grown on the island and there is an endless supply of fresh organic vegetables, bursting with flavour. The prawns, or gambas, which are caught in the Mediterranean, are the sweetest and best I have ever tasted.

The first time Juan cooked for us it was a sea bream, a large wild one that had been caught only a few hours earlier just outside the port in front of the restaurant. Anna brought it whole to the table and served it to us, making sure we had a potato each and some oil and lemon to pour over. It was memorable.

At the fishmonger's 'One sea bream weighing 450 grams, scaled and gutted.' The sea bream most commonly found at your fishmonger's will be the daurade, otherwise known as the gilthead sea bream. It will be silver in colour with a dark nose and a gold stripe across it. Nearly all of them will have been farmed in France or Greece, and are perfectly acceptable, as are black or red bream.

You will need (serves 2) 2 potatoes, peeled and sliced into rounds about 1 cm thick — 1 × 450 g sea bream, scaled and gutted — a pinch of salt — 2 tomatoes, quartered — 1 teaspoon sugar — 2 cloves of garlic, peeled — a small handful of fresh parsley, finely chopped — a few glugs of good olive oil — a small handful of fresh breadcrumbs — lemons, for serving

---

To make Preheat the oven to its maximum temperature. Cook the potatoes in boiling water for 3–4 minutes. Lay the fish on a roasting tray and sprinkle with salt. Place the potatoes, tomatoes and garlic cloves around the fish, and sprinkle with a pinch of sugar and salt. Pour a few glugs of olive oil into the roasting dish; and scatter the breadcrumbs lightly over the top. Cover tightly with foil and bake in the preheated oven for 20 minutes, then remove the foil, sprinkle with parsley and bake for a further 5 minutes.

To serve This makes a great family supper. Serve everyone moist chunks of the fish, potato and tomato and then spoon the juices over the top. It really is delicious. Pass round chunks of lemon to squeeze over, and eat with a nice fresh salad and slices of lightly toasted bread rubbed with garlic and a cut tomato.

Try this too . . . Use other fish, such as sea bass or red mullet. Try using basil instead of parsley, or add a few extra cloves of garlic to the breadcrumbs. A few rinsed, salted capers or salted anchovies baked with the fish add something to the juice.

Fried Swordfish Milanese Style with Wild Oregano and Anchovy

One of my favourite dishes in almost any Italian restaurant is Veal milanese: thin slices of veal coated in breadcrumbs and fried, finished on your plate with loads of lemon juice. The inspiration for this dish came from it.

Swordfish is firm and has a wonderful texture. At first I ate it just thinly sliced, coated in fresh white breadcrumbs and lightly fried, but then I found that dried wild oregano and salted anchovy fillets mixed with the breadcrumbs really added something. It is easy to make and is delicious served with spaghetti tossed with a fresh tomato sauce. Try it.

At the fishmonger's 'Two thin slices of swordfish from a nice large loin.' With big swordfish the fillets, or loins, as they are called, can be several inches across. I think these are the best, as a slice almost covers the whole plate. If only smaller loins are available just use more slices.

You will need (serves 2) 6 salted anchovy fillets — a chunk of 1–2 day old bread — 1 level tablespoon wild dried oregano (on the branch if possible) — 2–4 thin slices of swordfish — a few tablespoons plain flour — 1 egg, beaten — vegetable oil for frying — 1 lemon

---

To make Put the anchovy fillets, bread and oregano into the food processor and whiz until you have fine crumbs. Dip the swordfish into first the flour, then the egg and lastly the breadcrumb mixture. Pour some vegetable oil into a hot, heavy-based frying pan, give it a few minutes to get to a good hot temperature and then carefully lay the swordfish into the pan and fry gently for 3–4 minutes either side until the crumb is a nice crisp golden brown. Before putting on serving plates finish with a good squeeze of lemon.

To serve A Caprese salad with ripe tomatoes and mozzarella (see page 44) is a perfect accompaniment, as is a bowl of haricot beans dressed with olive oil, garlic, sea salt and parsley.

Try this too ... Add some sun-dried tomatoes or pine nuts to the breadcrumbs to give a different flavour, or maybe some garlic or chilli. This way of cooking would also work well with marlin, tuna and mackerel fillets. Fry them gently in good olive oil, then remove from the pan and keep warm. Add some sliced garlic to the pan, fry until crisp, and squeeze in some lemon juice to make a sauce.

Grilled Monkfish with Rosemary and Caprese Salad

There is nothing like a properly made Caprese salad: sweet tomatoes, fragrant basil and as-fresh-as-you-can-get-it creamy bufala mozzarella, dressed simply with olive oil. It goes fantastically well with grilled fish, and monkfish is a good one for the barbecue. This way of cooking monkfish gives it the little extra flavour it needs and its texture stands up well to a hot grill. Take a few long, thin slices of monkfish fillet and thread them on to a rosemary skewer before chucking them on to the barbecue or grill. It's great with this simple, delicious salad.

At the fishmonger's 'One monkfish tail, weighing about 500–600 grams, filleted, with the skin and membrane removed.' Get your fishmonger to do the fiddly job of removing the monkfish membrane. This is the pinkish stuff on the outside of the fish that will turn black and make the fish curl when cooked. It won't harm you, it just doesn't look too good.

You will need (serves 4) 500–600 g monkfish, filleted and skinned — 8 sprigs of fresh rosemary (kept long for skewering) — 100 g tomatoes per person (plum, vine, cherry or a mixture) — 2 bufala mozzarellas, weighing 125 g each — a handful of whole, fresh, bushy basil leaves — good extra virgin olive oil — a squeeze of lemon juice — sea salt

To make Slice the monkfish thinly lengthways down each fillet and cut into 8 lengths. Thread a sprig of rosemary through each one until the whole strip is skewered.

Slice the tomatoes, leaving the smaller ones whole. Arrange on a serving plate with torn-up chunks of mozzarella. Scatter the fresh basil leaves on top and dress with your best extra virgin olive oil. Lemon-flavoured oil works well too.

Get your grill or barbecue hot. Brush the monkfish with a little oil and a sprinkle of sea salt and grill for 2–3 minutes per side, allowing the fish to lightly char and the rosemary to blacken.

Place the monkfish on top of the salad and finish with a further sprinkling of crunchy sea salt, a squeeze of lemon and a little more olive oil.

To serve This is a great main course or starter, or you can serve it in one big bowl with the monkfish scattered over the top and let everyone dive in.

Try this too ... Try a mixture of green and red tomatoes, purple and green basil and other fresh herbs that are your favourites. Sprinkle a few dried chilli flakes into the olive oil before dressing the salad. A bit of sliced garlic or salted anchovy popped into the fish with the rosemary also works well. If you think the flavour of your tomatoes is not zingy enough, try this: cut in half (leave cherry tomatoes whole) and roast them in a very low, and I mean low, oven with a bit of olive oil and a sprinkling of sugar for 4 or 5 hours, then leave them to go cold. You can do a big batch and store them in Kilner jars.

Grilled Tuna with Oregano, Oil, Lemon and Sea Salt

The best piece of tuna I have eaten was earlier this year when my son Ben and I had a week away in Menorca. We spent the whole week doing what boys do and topped it off on the last day by chartering a boat and a skipper to take us out fishing for yellow-fin tuna. About twenty-five miles off the coast we had our first catch, and by the end of the day we had five magnificent fish.

We were leaving at eight the next morning and there wasn't time for a last meal or barbecue. But I was not going to leave that boat without taking at least one fish, so we cut it into loins and carted it away in carrier bags packed with the ice cubes that had kept our beer cold. I kept it in the fridge overnight and in the morning some of our clothes and towels were discarded and the tuna was packed between carrier bags filled with ice for the flight.

Three hours later we were home. When I opened the suitcase just about everything was bloodstained but the tuna was still cold to touch with the back of my hand and I didn't care!

The flavours in this dish are typical of the Mediterranean. Mix the smell of those flavours with warm air and you can transport yourself to any table outside any restaurant on the Italian coast. It is a pungent mix which works well as a dressing with almost any grilled fish, best of all when it's been cooked over a fire outdoors. I like it with tuna, as it stands up to these sorts of flavours. Once made, the dressing will keep well in the fridge.

At the fishmonger's 'Four tuna steaks weighing 175 grams each, from the thick end of the fish.' Swordfish and marlin also work well cooked and served this way.

You will need (serves 4) 1 teaspoon sea salt — juice of 1 lemon — a small handful of fresh oregano, chopped, or a tablespoon of dried (on the branch if possible) — 4–5 tablespoons good, fruity olive oil — 4 × 175 g tuna steaks — freshly ground black pepper

---

To make Make the dressing by dissolving the salt in the lemon juice, then stir in the oregano. Gradually add the olive oil to make a dressing. Preheat your grill for about 10 minutes before you start to cook, and preheat the oven to 200°C/400°F/gas 6. Lightly brush the tuna steaks with olive oil, season with freshly ground black pepper, and grill for 2–3 minutes either side until nicely charred but pink and warmed through in the centre. If your steaks are thick or if you like your tuna well done, put them into the preheated oven for 2–3 minutes, being careful not to overcook them.

To serve Prick the fish with a fork a few times and rub the dressing in with the back of a spoon. Put the tuna on a plate and drizzle the rest of the dressing over and around it. A lovely side dish to make while the grill is hot is grilled onions with halloumi, walnuts and mint (see page 180). If you don't have any halloumi, just lightly grill a few slices of red onion and dress them with the walnut and mint dressing.

Try this too ... Add chilli flakes to the dressing, or replace the oregano with dried sage and a chopped red onion.

Sautéd Spider Crab with Garlic, Lemon and Parsley

There are some good full-on flavours in this dish. It's messy to eat and you have to fight a bit for your food, but the pleasure of sucking, licking and chewing every last drop of rich, salty, garlicky butter from the crab shell is enough to make you want to try this one. Brown crabs can be used, but I think spider crabs, which are so much cheaper anyway, look much more funky, and are delicious and sweet.

At the fishmonger's 'One cooked spider crab, about a kilo in weight.' It should feel heavy for its size and smell of nothing but the beach. You'll be filling yourself up on the bread which is dunked in the juices at the bottom of the crab, as well as the crab meat, so don't look at the crab and wonder how it is going to feed 4, get an extra loaf in! To cook a live spider crab, see page 66.

You will need (serves 2) 1 cooked spider crab — 100 g good garlic butter (see page 28) — a splash of white wine — a pinch of sea salt — a handful of chopped fresh parsley — a squeeze of lemon juice

---

To make Turn the spider crab on its back and with your thumbs against the back of the underside of the shell, push upwards so you have the top shell in one hand and the body and legs in the other. Remove the 'dead men's fingers', which look like little pointed triangular feathers. Drain the liquid and brown meat from the shell (keep this – there won't be very much) and with your fingers pull out any plastic-looking membrane and discard. To remove the stomach, have the back shell of the crab facing upwards, place your thumb just behind the crab's eyes and mouth and press downwards until you hear a click. Pull the stomach from the crab and discard. Pop the top shell in a very low oven to warm, as it will be used for serving the crab in. Twist off the claws, give them a good crack with the back of a heavy knife, and cut the body into 6 pieces so that you have pieces of body with legs attached.

Melt the garlic butter in a pan. Add a splash of white wine, a good pinch of sea salt and half the parsley. When it is foaming and gently bubbling but not browning, add the pieces of crab and turn them to coat them completely in the pan juices. Place a lid on the pan and continue to cook gently for 8–10 minutes, turning the crab occasionally and making sure the butter does not burn. Lastly add the remaining parsley with a squeeze of lemon juice and the reserved juices from the crab. If there is a lot of liquid you may need to return the pan to the heat for a minute, to reduce.

To serve Remove the top shell from the oven – it should be just warm – and pile the crab pieces up inside the shell. Pour over the hot garlicky butter. If you need any more juice, quickly melt a little more garlic butter and finish it with lemon juice and some parsley. Serve with plenty of bread and put a bowl on the table for the shells.

Baked Shellfish with Bucatini, Whole Roasted Garlic and Thyme

Some of the best dishes I have ever cooked have been the spontaneous ones. This was one of those dishes. I had some shellfish left over from another recipe, a handful of bucatini from the crab dish on page 66, some thyme, some big, fat bulbs of garlic, we were hungry, and it turned out just brilliant. Here it is.

At the fishmonger's 'A good handful of mussels, half a dozen small, raw shell-on prawns, three or four langoustines, 50 grams of squid and a handful of clams.' This is a really flexible recipe and you can use almost any shellfish, but make sure you include mussels or clams, or both, because their juices are so good.

You will need (serves 3–4) 8 large cloves of garlic, unpeeled — 100 ml olive oil — salt — a splash of good white wine — a handful of mussels — 6 raw shell-on prawns — 3–4 langoustines — 50 g squid — a handful of clams — a handful of cooked bucatini pasta — a pinch of chilli flakes, or 2 very tiny hot red, dried chillies — 250 ml home-made tomato sauce or passata (use the rustic chunky variety) — 3–4 sprigs of fresh thyme

To make Preheat the oven to 150°C/300°F/gas 2. Put the cloves of garlic into a roasting tray with the olive oil and a pinch of salt, and roast in the preheated oven until softened, about 10–12 minutes. Remove from the oven and set aside to cool. Raise the oven temperature to 200°C/400°F/gas 6.

Lay out a square of tinfoil, large enough to hold all the ingredients and to be folded and sealed tightly into a parcel. Cut a piece of baking parchment the same size as the foil and lay it on top so you have a double layer. Add a splash of wine to the garlic in the roasting tray and add the shellfish, pasta and chillies. Toss everything together, place in a heap on the baking parchment, pour over the passata or tomato sauce, and lay the thyme sprigs on top. Fold it up to make a tightly sealed parcel, place on a roasting tray and bake in the oven for 25 minutes.

To serve Place the whole thing in the middle of the table, get your noses round the top of the parcel as you open it up, pull the sides of the foil apart, give it a mix around, put a few wedges of lemon on top and get stuck in.

Spaghetti with Sardinian Bottarga, Lemon and Parsley

If you have never come across bottarga before then you *must* find yourself a good Italian delicatessen and buy some. It is delicious, with a really unusual flavour which seems to change as you are eating it, leaving your mouth tingling with the fresh flavour of the seaside. Bottarga is made from the roe of grey mullet, a fish which isn't always given enough credit. I think it is delicious. Whether you like the fish or not, the roe prepared in this way is out of this world. I think Sardinian bottarga is the best.

I like the way it melts and coats the pasta with the lemon and parsley, adding an extra bit of freshness. You can also slice it thinly, drizzle it with the best olive oil, and eat it as an appetizer or simply as a treat. Because it's dried it keeps for a long time. A potato peeler is ideal to make thin shavings, just as you would with parmesan.

At the fishmonger's Only a few select fishmongers will stock bottarga. You can buy it from any good Italian delicatessen or by mail order from *fishworks.co.uk*. It's expensive, but a little goes a long way.

You will need (serves 2) good olive oil — 2 tablespoons grated bottarga — sea salt — a couple of handfuls of cooked spaghetti — zest of ½ a lemon and juice of 1 — a handful of fresh parsley, chopped

---

To make Put the olive oil in a wide frying pan over a gentle heat – if it is too hot the bottarga will fry and the flavour will spoil. Add the bottarga (keeping a little to one side to add at the end) and just a pinch of sea salt, then add your cooked pasta and toss it all together, making sure that everything is well mixed. When it is hot enough to serve, add the lemon zest and the parsley, sprinkle over the lemon juice and give it a final toss, then sprinkle over the reserved bottarga.

Try this too . . . Try using a lemon-infused olive oil instead of the lemon juice, replacing the lemon zest with orange zest and adding just a touch of fresh mint.

Lobster, Crab and Rice Stew

This recipe is based upon the famous Menorcan lobster calderata, a simple stew made from spiny lobsters or langoustes, which are caught all around the Mediterranean. It makes a wonderful centrepiece for a Sunday lunch. You can pick out a piece of crab or lobster, crack it, suck it, chew it, drink the juice and then spoon the creamy rice into your bowl – the whole thing is an experience.

At the fishmonger's 'One live lobster, about 500 to 600 grams, and one live hen crab, about the same weight.' You can use cooked lobster and crab, but I don't think the flavour is the same. If you see small velvet crabs at the fishmonger's, add a couple, and if you are lucky enough to see a nice crawfish throw that in instead of the lobster.

You will need (serves 4-6) 1 live lobster — 1 live crab — olive oil — 2 medium onions, finely sliced — 2 green peppers, deseeded and cut into strips — 4 plump cloves of garlic, finely chopped — 500 g good ripe plum or vine tomatoes, roughly chopped — a large handful of fresh parsley, chopped — 1 wineglass of brandy — 1 large wineglass of white wine — 2 handfuls of paella rice — sea salt

---

To make First prepare the shellfish. Kill the lobster by putting the point of a sharp knife on the back of the head, giving the handle a downward thump with the flat of your hand and then levering the knife towards the end of the tail so that it is cut in half. Turn the lobster through 180 degrees and separate the head end in half too. Spoon out the creamy brown meat and roe from the head section of the shell and reserve. Twist off the claws, give them a good crack and chop the rest of the lobster into chunks. Do not throw away the head shells. Don't be put off by anything green, this is the roe of the lobster and will turn red when cooked.

To kill the crab, see page 66. Once the crab is dead remove the top shell and with your thumb, press down just behind the eyes until you hear a click. Remove the stomach, and pick out any plastic-looking membrane. Pull off the 'dead men's fingers' which are attached to the body – they look like feathers and are obvious. Scrape everything else from the inside of the shell into a bowl. I know you won't feel at all appetized by what you see but don't worry – this is just uncooked brown meat and perhaps some soft shell, which when the crab is boiled turns into what we know as the brown meat. You need this to add to the richness, so please don't throw it away. With the heel of the knife cut each leg at the last joint before the pointed claw-like bit at the end and throw that bit away. Then cut the body into eight pieces so that each leg has a chunk of the body still at the end – this is great for picking out and sucking.

Heat a few tablespoons of olive oil in a large heavy pan, big enough to take all the ingredients and a few pints of water, and very gently soften the onions and green peppers – this will take about 15–20 minutes. Add the garlic, tomatoes and half the parsley, and cover. When everything has cooked to a creamy paste, add the brandy and allow it to boil for a couple of minutes, then add the wine and do the same. Add the pieces of crab and lobster, stir and then add 565 ml of water. Cover and simmer gently for about 45 minutes, checking every so often to make sure the pan doesn't dry out – if it does, just add a little more water. Then add the rice, cover and cook for a further 20 minutes. Stir in the remaining parsley before serving.

Surf Clam and Parsley Risotto

I simply adore risotto. It has inspired a whole load of new dishes for me. The rules are simple, but it does need attention while cooking – you have to stir the rice constantly, My friend Franz in Venice told me always to stir in the same direction, to massage the creamy starches from the rice and give it the luxurious texture that comes from the rice itself and not from added cream. I love the way it just holds together. The consistency of risotto varies in different parts of Italy: in Venice they serve it wetter, which is how I prefer it – with a wave.

You have to use good rice – I find carnaroli the best. It is longer and flatter and really absorbs the flavours it is cooked with.

At the fishmonger's 'One and a half kilos of surf clams.' If surf clams aren't available then use palourdes, otherwise known as carpet clams (their shells are a little thicker so you may want to buy a few more, and they will be more expensive but delicious), or soft shell clams. If there are any razor clams to be had I steam those open with the others and chop up the meat. Avoid the clams called amandes – they are too tough. If you can't get fresh clams use a tin of baby clams, using the liquid as stock.

You will need (serves 4) 1.5 kg clams — 1 wineglass of dry white wine — 25 g unsalted butter — 1 onion, finely chopped — 3 large cloves of garlic, finely chopped — 300 g carnaroli rice — 1 small dried hot chilli — a handful of fresh parsley — water — salt

To make Put the clams into a pan with a tight-fitting lid and add most of the wine. Cover, turn up the heat, and cook until all the clams have opened. Discard any that don't. Remove the clams from their shells and set aside. Reserve the liquid, straining it if you think it may be sandy.

In a heavy-based sauté pan, melt the butter and add the onion and garlic. Fry gently for about 10–12 minutes, until softened, then add the rice. Stir the rice gently until it is translucent. Crumble the chilli over the top, then add a splash more white wine and allow it to be absorbed and evaporated. Gradually add, a little at a time, the warmed reserved juice from the clams and half the parsley. Add hot water, a ladleful at a time, stirring gently with a wooden spoon in the same direction until the rice is cooked and creamy. This will take about 20 minutes.

Lastly add the meat from the clams and the remaining parsley, season with salt, and cook for a further 2–3 minutes. Cover the pan, remove from the heat, whisk in a knob of butter and let the risotto stand for a further couple of minutes. The texture should be creamy and pourable.

To serve I enjoy risotto either as the main part of a meal or in a smaller quantity as a starter. It works really well when lots of people are eating together. Serve in wide shallow bowls.

Try this too ... Use cockles instead of clams and fry finely diced pancetta with the onions at the beginning. Or use mussels and a pinch of saffron.

Taramasalata or Tarama

This Greek dish is traditionally made with grey mullet roe, but smoked cod's roe is more commonly used now. This recipe makes something completely different from the bright pink stuff sold in supermarkets. Serve it with croûtons, black olives and maybe a few ripe or roasted tomatoes.

Once made it will keep for 3–4 days in the fridge.

At the fishmonger's '250 grams of smoked cod's roe.' Look for roe that is soft and creamy with a sweet smoky smell. Its colour will range from dark orange to pale pink, but the colour doesn't matter, just make sure it is not hard and overcooked as this will not make good tarama.

You will need (makes enough for 6–8 servings) 2 slices of yesterday's bread, crusts removed — 1–2 cloves of garlic — juice of 1 lemon — 250 g smoked cod's roe — 300 ml vegetable oil — 100 ml olive oil — ½ a wineglass of cold water

---

To make Put the bread and garlic into a food processor and switch on, adding lemon juice until you have a smooth paste. Then add the cod's roe, including the skin, which I think contains a lot of the flavour as it has been in direct contact with the smoke in the kiln. Keep blitzing until the mixture is smooth and creamy then add the vegetable oil in a gentle stream until you have a thick buttery consistency. Slowly add the olive oil – you may find it becomes quite stiff and cloying but don't worry – then add the water slowly until you get the right consistency, if you add too much and the mixture becomes too sloppy, simply drizzle in more oil until you get it right.

To serve I serve this in bowls, sprinkled with chopped parsley or coriander, maybe a few finely chopped black olives and a glug of good fruity olive oil. It is also good with a small finely chopped onion mixed in. For dipping I like to use slices of bread which have been brushed with oil and toasted on a barbecue or grill plate, or a denser, harder bread like sourdough.

Try this too . . . Mix a few tablespoons of tarama into some warm cooked spaghetti with parsley, mint and lemon juice.

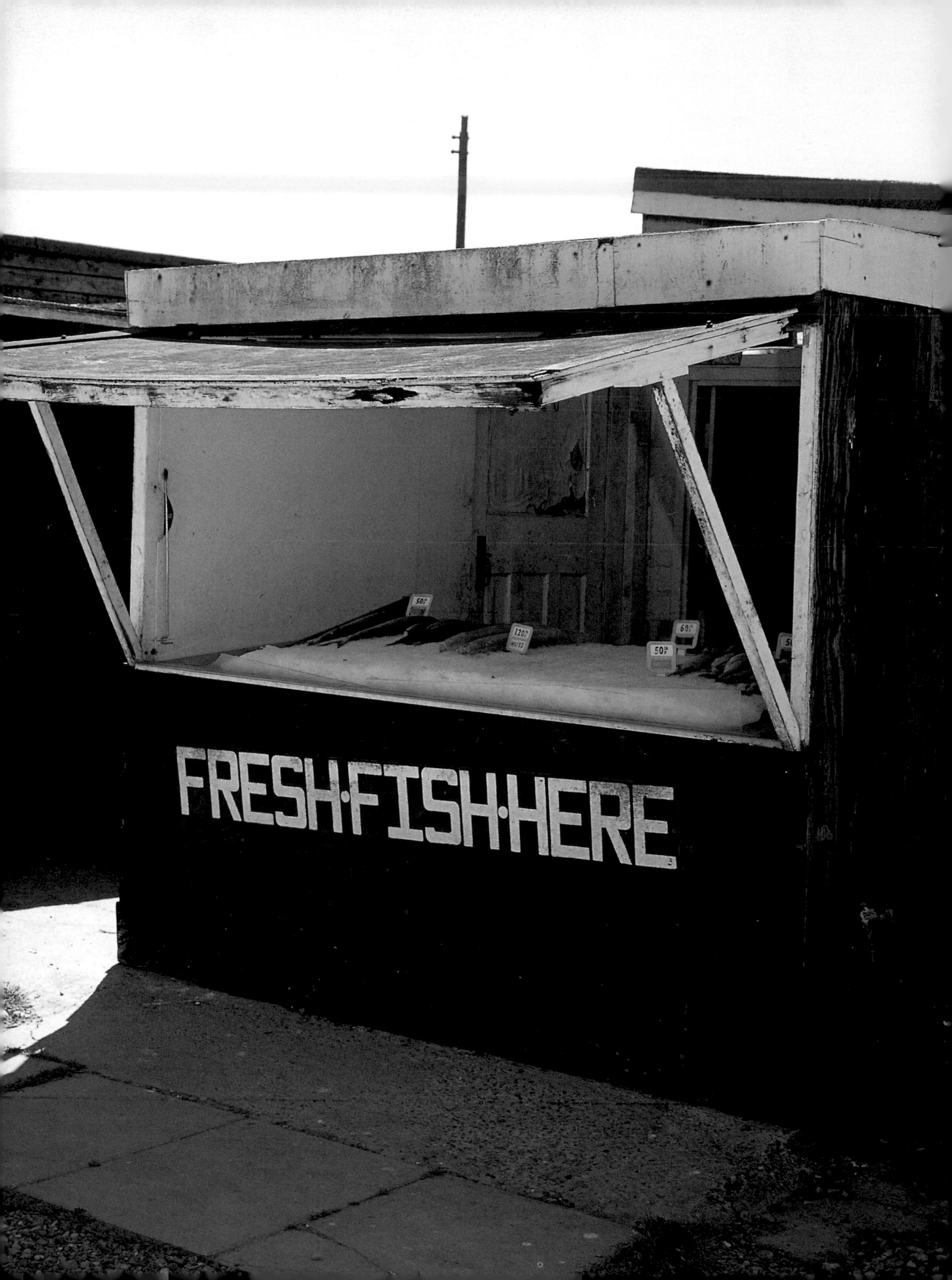
FRESH·FISH·HERE

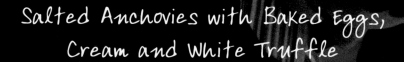

Salted Anchovies with Baked Eggs, Cream and White Truffle

What a fantastic combination this is! I was given this recipe by my Italian friend Norbert, who is a winemaker in Piedmont, northern Italy. We met when we shared a dinner table and discovered the same love for food and wine. During our conversation he became excited about truffles, as it was the height of the season back home, and he gave me this recipe. I was intrigued and excited, so I met him in Piedmont, ate it, brought some truffles home and made it – it was delicious. I don't expect you to rush out and buy white truffles – the combination of anchovies and eggs is so good that a bit of truffle oil is perfectly acceptable. However, a fresh truffle might come your way one day, so remember this simple recipe. This is how Norbert gave me the instructions: 'Put the red of two eggs in a small dish, two tablespoons of cream on top, one teaspoon of bagna cauda [salted anchovies melted with butter, garlic and olive oil], put it in a hot oven [200°C/400°F/gas 6] for a couple of minutes until the first bubbles come to the top, then take it out, whisk it with a fork so it is still creamy and runny and slice white truffle over the top.' I can't think of a better way to describe how to make it.

Creamy Salt Cod with Onions, Mozzarella and Parsley

I have definitely got a thing about salt cod. I cook it now more than ever, and I am always trying out new things. This dish is comfort food at its best. Serve it with lots of bread to scoop up the sauce.

If you like salt cod, get into the habit of salting your own – it is simple, and well worth the effort. If you are salting cod especially for this dish, you will need to start 1–2 days in advance.

At the fishmonger's 'One cod fillet, about 600 grams, skinned and bones removed.' To salt and soak it, see page 36. You can buy ready-salted cod but it is generally too dry and requires too much soaking.

You will need (serves 4) 1 onion, finely sliced — olive oil — 3 cloves of garlic, crushed to a paste — a splash of white wine — 750 ml béchamel sauce (see page 20) — 600 g salt cod, soaked and ready to cook — 100 ml single cream — a good handful of fresh parsley, finely chopped — freshly ground black pepper — 2 or 3 bufala mozzarellas, 125 g each — 1–2 lemons

---

To make In a saucepan large enough to hold all the ingredients, very gently fry the onion in a little olive oil until soft and almost melted; this will take 15–20 minutes. If the onions start to brown at the edges, add a little water to cool the pan down and help them soften. Add the garlic and cook for another 3–4 minutes. Add the white wine and allow it to reduce down to a tablespoon or so, then stir in the béchamel, which should be the consistency of double cream.

Break the salt cod into pieces, making sure there are no bones (you will feel these with your fingers), and add it, piece by piece, to the onion sauce. Continue to cook gently for 4–5 minutes until the cod starts to flake, then add the cream, most of the parsley and plenty of black pepper. Pour the mixture into a heatproof dish that you can put under the grill and take to the table. Break the mozzarella into chunks with your hands and lay it on top. Pop the whole thing under a preheated grill until the cheese is melted and the top bubbling. Finish with a good turn of black pepper, a final sprinkling of parsley and a squeeze of lemon juice.

To serve Put the dish in the middle of the table with a bowl of good olive oil, some lemon wedges and plenty of bread or chunks of raw vegetables.

Try this too ... If you have any left over this is delicious cold. Or you can just spread it on toast and warm it under the grill with sliced tomatoes, a few torn basil leaves and a drizzle of olive oil. Or stir a couple of tablespoons into some mashed potato to serve with a bit of your favourite grilled or smoked fish. It is ideal for topping crostini to serve before dinner. Try adding a few chopped cornichons for an extra twist.

Good salt cod can be thinly sliced and served raw with lemon juice, olive oil and parsley. Try it!

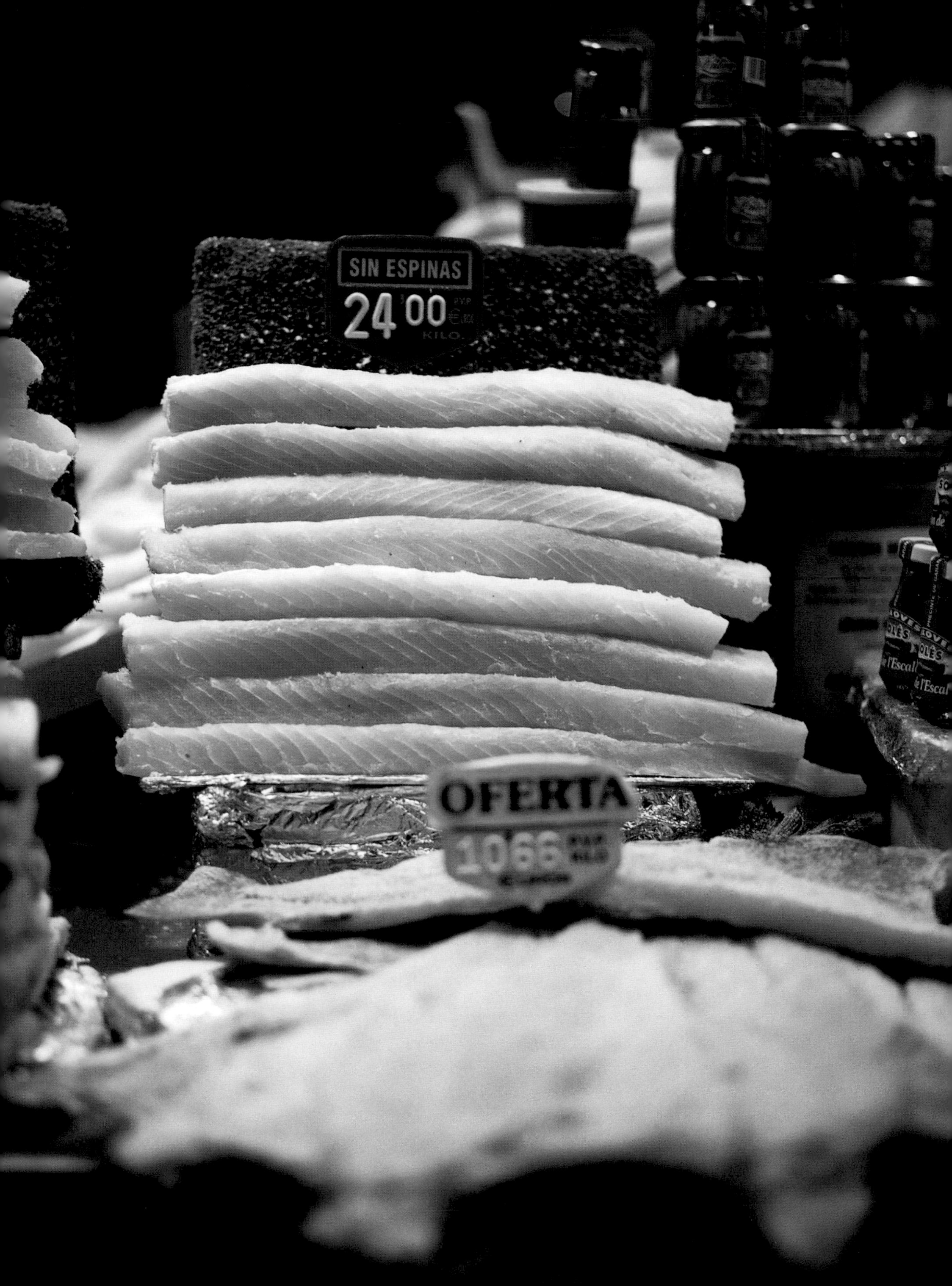
SIN ESPINAS
24 00
KILO
OFERTA

Salt Cod Cream

Leftover salt cod can be transformed into something spectacular. Once this is made it will keep for a few days in the fridge and is ideal to use for topping canapés. Or just spread thickly on fresh cut bread, drizzle with olive oil, sprinkle with chopped black olives and put under the grill for a few minutes until it bubbles and browns.

You will need (serves 4–6 as a dip) 200 ml milk — 1 bay leaf — 150 g salt cod, soaked and ready to cook (see page 36) — 2 egg yolks — 1 plump clove of garlic — 2 tablespoons water — 100 ml vegetable oil — 50 ml good olive oil

---

To make Bring the milk to a gentle simmer and add the bay leaf. Put in the salt cod and allow it to poach for 3–4 minutes until cooked, then remove it from the pan and drain. Put the egg yolks, garlic and water into a food processor and blitz until the egg yolks are white. Add the salt cod and continue to blitz to a smooth paste. With the motor still running, drizzle in vegetable oil and olive oil until you get a smooth, creamy consistency. If it is too stiff a little water will loosen it up; if it is too wet, continue to add more oil. Use more vegetable oil than olive oil as the flavour of the latter may be too strong. In this dish it is just there to flavour and not take over. When you have got it right the consistency should be like light whipped cream.

Try this too ... This has a light consistency, almost like mayonnaise. Try a tablespoonful on top of a tomato, onion and basil salad.

Fried Herring Roes on Toast with Anchovy, Rosemary and Gherkins

These make a lovely snack or a delicious canapé. You can also use Gentleman's Relish, instead of the flavoured butter, coat the herring roes in flour, beaten egg and breadcrumbs, and either deep or shallow fry them.

At the fishmonger's '150 grams of fresh soft herring roes.' The herring has both hard and soft roe, the soft variety being called the milts. I think they are the best as they are more creamy. The hard roes are more grainy and they are usually only sold defrosted.

You will need (serves 2) 150 g soft herring roes — plain flour — butter for frying — 2 pieces of toast — 25 g anchovy and rosemary butter (see page 28) or a little Gentleman's Relish — 6 small gherkins, finely sliced — a squeeze of lemon juice — 1 tablespoon chopped fresh parsley

---

To make Lightly coat the roes in flour and fry gently in a little butter for 3–4 minutes until golden. Spread the toast with the anchovy and rosemary butter or Gentleman's Relish and lay the gherkins on top. Add a good squeeze of lemon juice to the herring roes, sprinkle with the parsley, then lay the roes on top of the toast and serve.

Try this too ... Spread 2 more pieces of toast with the butter and put them on top of the roes, pressing down slightly so that the roes squash and ooze. Cut into small squares and spike with a cocktail stick. A little paprika or a teaspoon of roasted salt and pepper (see page 111) added to the flour makes a difference.

Pasta and Rice with Seafood

Pasta with fish has become one of my favourite things to cook. It's easy, quick, flexible and above all delicious; sounds perfect, doesn't it? Some good olive oil, a clove of garlic, a few chunks of fresh lobster and some pine nuts, all tossed together with spaghetti, sea salt, lemon and fresh pungent basil leaves – I love it!

I like to serve pasta dishes family-style – just put a big bowl on the table and get everybody helping themselves. Put a few fresh salads on the table too, and a bottle of good olive oil for drizzling on your food. Dishing up in one bowl is so easy and you have time to add those extra little touches like a sprinkling of sea salt, extra herbs, black pepper or lemon juice, which can really make a difference.

Simple things like a few mussels, a bashed clove of garlic and a handful of parsley can make enough of a sauce to give a bowl of spaghetti a fresh, sea-tasting flavour. Pasta tops the flexibility charts: a chopped chilli will add a bit of heat, coriander will change the flavour altogether and lemon juice will add a final zing. I always like a fresh taste and 'crunchy' texture to my pasta dishes, to show off all the ingredients at their best. Just imagine sweet prawns, the first of the fresh peas, mint and good oil. You just know it is fresh, seasonal and healthy and that it is going to taste good.

You don't have to stick to spaghetti, tagliatelle and macaroni – if you go to a good Italian supplier there are endless shapes and sizes to choose from, and they all have their own character. My favourite supplier is La Bottega in Bath, run by a lovely Sicilian family who are always so helpful and love sharing their recipes. 'Fresh' pasta has become popular, and people often think fresh is better than dried, but I disagree. Although making your own fresh pasta is a pleasure, and good therapy a few times a year, it is not a necessity. I still prefer dried pasta from producers like La Molisana, who make over 100 different shapes and regional specialities and have been producing pasta for Italians since 1911, which is good enough for me. I think it is the best, but you will find a brand that suits you. Italian ones, I think, will always be better.

Bucatini with Spider Crab, Pine Nuts, Fresh Tomato and Herbs

Spider crabs are not eaten in Britain as much as they should be, and many of the crabs landed here end up on the tables of France and Italy. I think part of the reason is that they are quite scary-looking chaps. The yield is much lower than with other crabs but the white meat from the claws, legs and body is sweet and delicious. During August and September hen crabs are in season, and when they are cooked you will often find lots of lumpy red roe which is delicious thrown in at the same time as the crabmeat.

At the fishmonger's 'One spider crab, weighing around one and a half kilos.' You can buy them live or cooked. If you buy yours live, cook it as soon as possible. Drop the crab into a large pan of boiling water with a good handful of sea salt and boil for 10–15 minutes. Remove the crab and stand it on its nose with cold water running over it for a further 5 minutes. If you can only get a cooked spider crab, make sure that it feels heavy for its size, then turn it over, pull back the flap and give it a sniff. It should smell of nothing but the beach – any other strong or ammoniac whiffs will mean you should avoid it. If spider crab isn't available, you can use a native brown crab or fresh white crab meat.

You will need (serves 4) 1 × 1.5 kg spider crab, live or cooked — good extra virgin olive oil — sea salt — 1 large clove of garlic, peeled and bashed — 1 tablespoon pine nuts — ½ a small shallot, finely chopped — 6 cherry tomatoes, cut into quarters — 150–200 g cooked bucatini or spaghetti — a small handful of fresh chervil — a small handful of fresh basil leaves, finely chopped — a squeeze of lemon juice — freshly ground black pepper

---

To make Remove the legs and claws from the crab. Snap a couple of the legs in half, then pick out the white meat from the rest. Tools that you might find useful are nut or shell crackers, a small hammer, and a pick or knitting needle. Put the olive oil into a pan with a good pinch of sea salt over a gentle heat. Add the garlic and the reserved crab legs and fry gently for 2–3 minutes, shaking the pan occasionally to make sure the oil is well flavoured, then remove the garlic and discard. Add the pine nuts and the shallot, then the tomatoes and pasta. Stir gently for a few minutes. Toss around, ensuring that the pasta is well coated with everything in the pan, then add the crab. Finish with the fresh herbs, a good squeeze of lemon and a sprinkling of freshly ground black pepper.

To serve I like to serve this at the table, straight from the pan. It also looks wonderful piled back into the top shell of the crab, washed and warmed through in a low oven.

Linguine with Scallops, Artichokes and Walnuts

Walnuts and pasta go really well together. I like to use fresh artichoke bottoms – they can be fiddly to prepare, but are worth the trouble. If you can't get them fresh, use tinned, or the grilled artichoke hearts which are sometimes available.

At the fishmonger's 'Four large diver-caught scallops.' The scallops must be dry – if they are sitting in water, or have been frozen, give them a miss and use clams or small slices of monkfish instead.

You will need (serves 2) 2 artichoke bottoms, cut into quarters — 50 ml olive oil — 25 g walnuts — 2 tablespoons mascarpone cheese — 50 ml double cream — 1 clove of garlic — 150 g cooked linguine — a handful of fresh parsley, chopped — juice of ½ a lemon — sea salt and freshly ground black pepper — 4 scallops, each cut in half to give 2 round discs

To make Fry the artichoke bottoms gently in olive oil until softened. Put the walnuts, mascarpone, cream and garlic into a food processor and blitz until smooth. Add this mixture to the pan and warm over a gentle heat, then add the pasta, parsley and lemon juice. Season with sea salt and freshly ground black pepper. Meanwhile, brush the scallops lightly with a little oil and season. Heat a frying pan until hot and sear the scallops on either side for about a minute and a half, until nice and golden. Place the scallops on top of the pasta and serve.

Add more lemon juice if you like, and season with freshly ground black pepper.

Try this too ... Use Pecorino Romano instead of mascarpone. It is saltier and sharper, so go easy with it. Fresh mint is great thrown in too.

Spaghetti with Clams, Olive Oil and Parsley

Clams – even the names sound appetizing: surf clams, venus clams, butter clams, manillas, palourdes . . . Most commonly at your fishmonger you will find small, tan-coloured surf clams or striped palourdes, which I think are the best as they are juicy and delicious eaten straight from the shell with nothing more than a squeeze of lemon. If you can get a few small razor clams, put them in too. Treat them the same way.

At the fishmonger's 'Two good handfuls of live clams.' Larger clams, like palourdes, will have heavier shells and you may need to buy a few more but the meat inside will be fatter and juicier. If they are really big, get the fishmonger to open one for you and try it there and then. Avoid large brown amande clams as these are too tough.

You will need (serves 2) 100 ml really good extra virgin olive oil — 2 large cloves of garlic, crushed — 2 handfuls of clams — a handful of fresh parsley, chopped — a few handfuls of cooked spaghetti — 1 red chilli, thinly sliced

---

To make Put the oil into a pan over a gentle heat and add the garlic. Give it a good stir to ensure the oil is well flavoured. Add the clams and half the parsley and stir again, turning the clams over so they become coated in the oil and garlic. Cover the pan, turn the heat up slightly, and wait for the clams to steam open – they will release loads of fabulous juice into the pan. If the clams take some time to open, don't let them fry – just add a splash of water to create some steam to help them along. Remove from the heat, add the spaghetti, chilli and the remaining parsley, and toss together until the pasta is just warmed through. Serve.

Try this too . . . Steam the clams open in a little white wine. Add a handful of coriander leaves before tossing with the pasta, chilli and parsley. A few tablespoons of fresh tomato sauce are good as well.

...NISH PLAICE   12.00
E

THE WHOLE TABLE

~~SEABASS FOR 4   16.00PP~~

ILL FOR 4   15.00PP

PLAICE FOR 2/3/4   13.00PP

HELLFISH

ILED CREVETTES   6.90

V. FishWorks

* ~~RANGE OF DANCES SAME 6 SIDES~~
* SEARED YELLOWFIN TUNA STEAK W/ S...
* FILLET OF CORNISH PLAICE W/ BLACK B...
* ROASTED RED MULLET W/ SWEET PEPPER
* BAKED SWORDFISH W/ SAFFRON + WILD T...
* CHUNK OF WILD HALIBUT W/ BRAISED FEN...

* ~~HAKE STEAK W/ SWEET GARLIC + PARSL~~

* WHOLE ROASTED GURNARD W/ AFRICAN

LOBSTER PRICES

~~HALF LOBSTER~~   ~~16~~

~~WHOLE LOBSTER~~   ~~29~~

Spaghetti with Scampi, Fresh Mint and Coriander

Most langoustines (scampi) available in the UK have been either previously frozen or dipped in a chemical solution to prolong their shelf-life. The effect of this is that the meat loses much of its delicate sweetness and the texture is often like cotton wool. Fresh langoustines are a totally different experience. They are volatile creatures and do not last long out of the water, so they are transported to the restaurant or fishmonger in tubes inside boxes to protect them. If you buy them live they will probably die within an hour or two. To enjoy them at their best, eat them as soon as possible. If you get them home and they are still very lively, either kill them with a sharp knife through the back of the head as with a lobster (see page 54) or pop them into the freezer for half an hour. They will be expensive but well worth it.

At the fishmonger's 'Eight medium large langoustines, live if possible.'

You will need (serves 2) 8 langoustines — 50 ml olive oil — sea salt and freshly ground black pepper — ½ a measure of brandy — 300 ml tomato sauce (see page 20) — 2 handfuls of cooked spaghetti — a handful of fresh mint, chopped — a handful of fresh coriander, chopped — lemon wedges for serving

---

To make After killing them, prepare the langoustines by twisting the tail from the head and then peeling the shell away from the tail so that you are just left with the meat. Squeeze all of the contents from the head of the langoustine into your tomato sauce. Don't worry, this is delicious meat and roe. If, however, you don't fancy it, leave it out. The claws on larger fish contain lovely sweet meat, so just snap these off, crack them, and break them. They can go into the dish whole.

Warm the olive oil and a pinch of sea salt in a heavy-based wide pan. Add the langoustine tails and claws and fry gently, making sure they are cooking evenly and are coated in the oil and salt. Turn the heat up slightly and sprinkle in the brandy. Tilt the pan away from you and allow the gas flame to set fire to the brandy. Let it burn for no more than 5–10 seconds, then blow it out. If your cooker is electric, sprinkle the brandy into a hot pan and either set fire to it with a match or boil it to remove some of the harshness. Turn the heat down and stir in the tomato sauce. Let it warm through, then add the pasta and the fresh herbs and toss everything together.

To serve Take the pan to the table and serve in individual bowls with chunks of lemon and salt and freshly ground black pepper.

Try this too ... If you do manage to get live langoustines, splash out on as many as you can afford, boil them in salted water for 8–10 minutes, and cool them down for a few minutes under cold water. Peel the tails and dunk them in fresh mayonnaise. Place your mouth over the end of the head, give it a squeeze and suck out the delicious meat that is so often discarded. Delicious, and an experience not to be missed.

Spaghettini with Lobster, Basil Leaf, Pine Nuts and Garlic

The gentle cooking of the chunks of raw lobster gets the flavour and oils from the shell working with the rest of the ingredients – I think this is one of the best lobster and pasta dishes I have ever tasted. We eat it regularly during the summer months, when lobsters are plentiful. It is one of those recipes you can cook anywhere, like at a beach barbecue or on a boat. It makes an exciting change to the usual idea of outdoor cooking. All you need is a tub full of the ingredients, a pan, a chuck-away barbecue and a few cases of wine.

At the fishmonger's 'One live lobster, weighing 750 grams.' Native lobsters are best (my preference is for those caught around Falmouth and St Mawes, but you don't have to be that fussy). I don't think the Canadian lobsters are as good, but a lot of people like them. Ask the fishmonger to put the lobster in a box with some wet newspaper or seaweed, or wrap it in wet newspaper in a carrier bag, take it home and put it in the fridge.

You will need (serves 4) 1 lobster — olive oil — 3 cloves of good garlic, crushed to a fine paste — a small handful of pine nuts — 4 handfuls of cooked spaghettini — 2 good handfuls of fresh basil leaves — a handful of grated parmesan or pecorino cheese — juice of 1 lemon — sea salt — lemons for serving

---

To make To kill and prepare your lobster, see page 54.

Put the olive oil into a wide, heavy-based frying pan, placed over a medium heat. Add the garlic and the pine nuts and stir into the oil, taking care that they don't start to fry. Stir in all the lobster pieces, coating them in the oil. Continue to sauté very gently, without colouring the garlic, for about 10–12 minutes, turning the lobster occasionally. It will turn a deep red colour and wonderful smells will waft from the pan. Add the pasta and toss everything together.

Remove the pan from the heat, tear up the basil leaves and add them to the pan with the parmesan or pecorino, lemon juice and sea salt. Give it a final good mix and serve.

To serve Tuck some lemon halves into the pan so your guests can add another squeeze if they like, and put the whole thing on the table for everyone to get stuck into. One of the pleasures of this dish is using your fingers and your mouth to get every last bit of salty, garlicky flavour from the shell of the lobster.

Try this too ... Fresh langoustines and prawns split in half make a great substitute for lobster. A few chopped ripe tomatoes can be added to the pan at the beginning, and, for those who like aniseed, add a handful of tarragon.

Tagliatelle with Mussels, Saffron and Rocket

Mussels are made for pasta, as they contain so much juice. Once they have been steamed open, a little butter, saffron and some fresh herbs will make an instant sauce to mix in with your favourite pasta shape.

At the fishmonger's '500 grams of tightly closed live mussels.' Discard any that do not close when you tap them. I think wild mussels have a better flavour than farmed ones, and often the meat is fatter.

You will need (serves 2) 500 g mussels — good olive oil — 1 clove of garlic — 1 tomato, roughly chopped — a splash of dry white wine — a pinch of saffron — a small handful of fresh tarragon, finely chopped — freshly ground black pepper — 2 handfuls of cooked tagliatelle — a handful of rocket leaves

To make Wash the mussels gently in cold water and remove the 'beards' by giving them a gentle tug. Pour a little olive oil into a heavy-based pan with a tight-fitting lid. If you don't have a lid, use a chopping board or a plate, just so long as the pan can be covered. Add the garlic and tomato and sweat gently for 2–3 minutes until just softened. Add the wine, boil for a minute to take off some of the alcohol, then add the mussels. Cover the pan, turn the heat up slightly and wait for the mussels to steam open – this will take about 3–4 minutes. Remove the mussels from the pan, discarding any that have not opened, then add the saffron and a tablespoon more olive oil to the juices and simmer gently. You will see the saffron turning the juices a rich golden yellow. Remove half the mussels from their shells and add to the juices, then add the remaining unshelled mussels and the tarragon. Add the rocket and allow it to wilt. Season with freshly ground black pepper. Add the tagliatelle to the pan and toss it all together until the pasta is just warmed through.

To serve Cold Pinot Grigio or Muscadet is perfect with it.

Try this too . . . Use cockles or clams or a mixture of both. I think cockles are particularly good; they are so juicy. If you like a bit more of an aniseed flavour, try a dash of Pernod or Ricard instead of the wine.

Baked Rice with Velvet Crabs and Saffron

I like rice because it can soak up flavours. That is probably why it is so popular in Spain and groups of men take themselves off to the beach to make paella, for which there are lots of recipes. This dish is not quite paella but is similar, in that it has the richness of saffron and the wonderful intense flavour you get from baking velvet crabs, which are caught in abundance around our coast and end up back in Spain or France. If you ask your fishmonger to get you some he shouldn't have too much of a job, especially in the summer. In this recipe the rice becomes crisp and you get a delicious crust on the bottom of the dish.

At the fishmonger's 'A kilo of cooked velvet crabs.' If velvet crabs are not available then one cooked hen crab weighing about a kilo will be sufficient and can be used instead. The other alternative is small green shore crabs, which again your fishmonger should be able to get for you.

You will need (serves 4) 1 kg cooked crabs — 1 large onion, finely chopped — 2 cloves of garlic, finely chopped — 1 red pepper, finely diced — olive oil — a good pinch of saffron — 1 shot of brandy — a large wineglass of white wine — 200 g paella rice — 500 ml water — sea salt and freshly ground black pepper — a good handful of fresh parsley, finely chopped — 1 lemon

---

To make Take the top shells off the crabs, remove the dead men's fingers (see page 14), and put the top shell back on. That is all the preparation that is needed.

Preheat the oven to 150°C/300°F/gas 2.

In a pan that is suitable for oven and table, fry the onion, garlic and pepper gently in olive oil for 20 minutes until soft and lightly golden. Stir in the saffron, then add the brandy and either flame it or leave it to reduce to almost nothing. Add the wine and boil to reduce by half. Add the rice and the crabs and fry for a further 3–4 minutes. Pour in the water and cook on top of the stove until the rice is about three-quarters cooked – it will still have a bite to it. Try not to keep stirring it, as you want a nice crust to build up on the bottom (if you don't fancy that then stir it). Make sure there is enough moisture in the pan to finish cooking the rice, season with salt and freshly ground black pepper, then pop it into the preheated oven until the rice is cooked and creamy with a slight crust on top. Sprinkle with parsley, squeeze over the juice of a lemon and serve.

To serve This dish is served straight from the dish in which it was cooked, and the crabs will be soft enough to break with your hands and suck out the insides. The claws are worth crunching with your teeth – they might be small but they do contain delicious flavours.

Try this too ... This is good made with langoustines or large prawns instead of crab.

Seafood Risotto

Use a bit of everything for this simple risotto. Creamy rice and good, fresh seafood flavours with just a spike of chilli and fresh parsley are what make it so delicious.

At the fishmonger's 'One squid weighing 150 grams, cleaned, 400 grams of mussels, 400 grams of clams, 400 grams of cockles, two langoustines, eight shell-on prawns, 50 grams of peeled prawns and 100 grams of monkfish or gurnard fillet.' Include some white fish and some shellfish. You can use any selection of fish but make sure you have plenty of mussels, clams or cockles, or a mixture, as these will make the stock.

You will need (serves 4) 400 g mussels — 400 g clams — 400 g cockles — ½ a bottle of dry white wine — 1 × 150 g squid — 100 g monkfish or gurnard fillet — 2 langoustines — 25 ml olive oil — 1 onion, finely chopped — 2 cloves of garlic, finely chopped — 1 small dried hot chilli — 300 g carnaroli rice — 8 shell-on prawns — 50 g peeled prawns — a good handful of fresh parsley, finely chopped — 20 g unsalted butter — lemon juice — sea salt

To make Tug the beards from the mussels and put them into a pan with a tight-fitting lid, with the clams and cockles. Add three-quarters of the wine and steam the shellfish open. Discard any that remain closed. Strain, reserving the stock – keep it hot for adding later to the risotto. If you wish you can remove the meat from the shells, discarding them and keeping the meat for adding to the risotto. Slice the squid into very thin rings and roughly chop the tentacles. Cut the monkfish or gurnard into small pieces and split the langoustines in half.

Heat the olive oil in a large pan and cook the onion, garlic and crumbled chilli gently until softened. Add the rice and continue to fry until it is translucent. Pour in the remaining wine and allow it to evaporate and be absorbed by the rice. Add the squid and the monkfish or gurnard. Slowly add a ladleful of the hot stock from the mussels, a little at a time, and let it be absorbed by the rice. Continue to add stock and stir the rice. After 10 minutes add the langoustines and the shell-on prawns and continue to cook, adding a little more stock, for a further 5 minutes. Add the reserved meat from the mussels, clams and cockles, and the peeled prawns, and cook for a further 2–3 minutes. The consistency should be creamy and the rice firm, but not chalky in the middle – add a little water if you don't have quite enough stock. Add the parsley and remove from the heat. Whisk in the butter and leave to stand for 2 minutes before serving.

To serve Spoon the risotto into wide flat bowls, giving them a gentle shake from side to side until the risotto is level in the bowl with bits of the shellfish poking through the surface of the rice. Finish with a squeeze of lemon, a pinch of sea salt and a drizzle of olive oil.

Crab and Rocket Risotto

Try using South Devon crabs, they're the best, especially those caught around Dartmouth. This little beauty in the photograph opposite is a spider crab, which could also be used in this recipe.

At the fishmonger's 'One live or freshly cooked cock crab, weighing about one and a half kilos.' I have used a cock crab in this recipe as they yield so much more white meat than the hen crab, and I think white crab meat is best in a risotto like this. Too much brown meat can be a little rich and the texture is too sticky.

You will need (serves 4) for the risotto: 1 × 1.5 kg crab — 1 small onion, finely chopped — 2 small cloves of garlic, finely chopped — olive oil — 300 g carnaroli rice — 1 small glass of Manzanilla, or other dry sherry — a handful of fresh rocket leaves — 25 g butter — **for the stock:** 1 leek, finely sliced — 1 fennel bulb, chopped — 1 onion, sliced — the crab shells — 1 wineglass of brandy — 1 wineglass of white wine

---

To make If your crab is alive, see page 66. Remove the top shell and the dead men's fingers (see page 14). Grab a glass of wine and a bit of help and pick the meat from the crab, making sure you keep the shells. Mash the brown meat until it is creamy, then flake the white meat by rubbing it between your fingers or gently breaking it down with a fork.

To make the stock, fry the leek, fennel and onion until light and golden, then add the crab shells and fry for about 4–5 minutes. Add the brandy, allow the alcohol to evaporate, then add the wine. Boil for a minute, then add about 1.25 litres of water and boil gently without a lid for 45 minutes. Strain into another pan and keep warm.

Gently fry the onion and garlic in a little olive oil until soft, about 10–12 minutes, then add the rice and fry gently until it is well coated and translucent. Add the sherry, and stir the risotto with a wooden spoon until it has been absorbed. Then, a little at a time, still stirring, add the hot crab stock – you will need about 1 litre – until it has all been used and the rice is cooked; this will take about 20 minutes. If you need more liquid, use hot water. When the risotto is creamy and the rice tender, add most of the rocket and stir it in until it wilts, then add the brown and the white crab meat and continue stirring. If you have any crab roe, add this too. To finish the risotto, stir in the butter in small pieces, then cover and leave to stand for a few minutes before serving. You should be able to pour the risotto from the pan into bowls. It should not be thick and stodgy.

To serve Serve in wide, deep bowls with a couple of rocket leaves on top.

Try this too ... This dish works really well with spider crab or lobster. If you don't have the time to cook a fresh crab, buy white crab meat, which is often sold in packs, and use a good-quality vegetable stock cube. But add an extra 250 ml of water when you make up the stock, so the flavours of the stock cube don't take over.

Shrimp Risotto with Tarragon

Most of the flavour is created in the early stages of cooking a risotto. I like to gently fry, in a mixture of olive oil and butter, fresh raw shrimps (prawns) with lots of garlic so that the oil becomes rich and intensely flavoured. When the rice is added it takes on flavour from the oil.

At the fishmonger's 'A kilo of raw 60/80 size prawns.' The most common size of prawn your fishmonger will stock will be 16/20s, and these will be fine to use, but the small ones are sweeter. During the summer months, when crabs are plentiful and the fishermen have got plenty of pots safely at sea, they often catch small brown shrimps in their pots – these are a must if you see them and a few handfuls made into a dish like this are excellent. Small brown Morecambe Bay shrimps are excellent too, but they are only available cooked. They are cooked at sea because they don't last long after being caught.

You will need (serves 4) a glug of olive oil — 2 large cloves of garlic, crushed to a paste or finely chopped — sea salt and freshly ground black pepper — 1 kg raw prawns — 1 small onion, finely chopped — 1 wineglass of brandy — 300 g carnaroli or arborio rice — 1 wineglass of white wine — a small handful of fresh tarragon, chopped — 25 g butter

---

To make Cover the base of a heavy pan with a thin layer of olive oil. Add half the garlic and a pinch of sea salt, and sauté the prawns very gently in batches for 5–6 minutes until they are coloured a nice orange and are firm to the touch. When removing them from the pan, make sure none of the oil is dripped and wasted. Peel the heads from the shrimps and squeeze their contents into a small dish for adding later (don't worry – they contain good-flavoured dark meat, which adds to the risotto). Peel the shell from each prawn body and reserve the flesh for later. The shells can be discarded. Add a bit more oil to the pan, then the onion and remaining garlic, and continue to cook until softened. Pour in the brandy and cook until completely evaporated. Add the rice, season with salt and continue to fry gently until translucent, then add the wine and continue to stir until it has been absorbed and evaporated. Add the reserved meat taken from the heads of the prawns and half the tarragon.

Add hot water ladleful by ladleful, while still stirring the same way. You will need about 500–700 ml, depending on your rice, but just add enough to ensure that the rice is cooked until soft and creamy – about 20 minutes. Now add the prawns and the remaining tarragon. Cook for a further 2–3 minutes, season to taste with black pepper, whisk in the butter in small pieces and leave to stand for another couple of minutes before serving.

To serve This is a dish for summer, and some lightly battered and deep-fried courgette flowers are perfect to eat with it.

Try this too ... If you have a cooked lobster and want to make a simple lobster risotto, cut it into chunks, remove the meat and fry the shells gently at the beginning to extract their flavour.

White Fish and Broad Bean Risotto with Saffron and Parsley

This is a good dish for making the best of fish like whiting, pollack, gurnard and ling, whose flavour and texture are often considered inferior to other species. You can use a mixture of fish, or just one type.

At the fishmonger's 'A mixture of whole, gutted, white fish, with the scales and gills removed but with the heads left on, about a kilo in weight.' See what he recommends. Make sure he cleans them well, and remember to ask him to remove the gills. If you can only get one type of fish that will be fine.

You will need (serves 4) for the risotto: 100 g broad beans (use frozen if fresh aren't available) — 50 g butter — 1 onion, finely chopped — 3 cloves of garlic, finely chopped — a pinch of good-quality saffron — a large bunch of fresh parsley, chopped, plus extra for serving — 300 g carnaroli or arborio rice — salt — ½ a wineglass of white wine — **for the stock:** 1 onion, finely chopped — 1 small leek, chopped — 1 carrot, chopped — a small bunch of fresh thyme — olive oil — ½ a wineglass of white wine — 1 kg white fish

---

To make First make the stock. Gently fry the onion, leek, carrot and thyme in a little olive oil until softened. Add the glass of wine and boil for a minute to take off the alcohol. Add the fish, cover with water and simmer for 20–30 minutes. Allow to cool until comfortable to handle. Lift out the fish and pull all the flesh away from the bones. Strain the liquid through a sieve into a saucepan and with the back of a ladle, using a small circular motion, gently rub the fish and liquid through the sieve until it is all gone. You should have about 500–600 ml of good stock. It should be full of fish flakes and shreds, not clear. Keep this hot in a pan.

To skin the broad beans, blanch them in boiling water for 40 seconds. Strain, run them under cold water, then squeeze the beans gently out of their tough outer skins and set them aside.

Melt half the butter in a heavy-bottomed pan and gently fry the onions and garlic until they are softened. Add the saffron and half the parsley, then add the rice and continue to cook for a minute or two until it is translucent. Add a few pinches of salt. Add the wine and stir the risotto in the same direction with a wooden spoon until it has been absorbed. Then, little by little, while constantly stirring, add the hot stock until it has been absorbed by the rice. After about 20 minutes the rice should be cooked and the risotto creamy. If you need any more liquid, use hot water. Lastly add the broad beans and the remaining parsley and stir in gently. Whisk in the rest of the butter. Cover and leave to stand for 2 minutes before serving.

To serve Serve in wide, flat bowls and sprinkle with parsley – the yellow of the risotto and the green of the parsley is stunning. It needs nothing else with it, but you can serve it as an accompaniment to simple roasted or grilled fish like sea bass or halibut.

Try this too ... Make a stock by steaming open 1 kg of mussels in a large glass of white wine. Remove the meat from the shells, and use the stock and more water if needed to cook the risotto. Add the mussel meat at the end – this will make you a mussel, saffron, broad bean and parsley risotto, which is a great combination too.

Easy Everyday Seafood

The recipes in this chapter are for dishes you can eat every day, dishes that always please. Nothing rich or fussy – the stuff you cook for all the family. Children are the most honest critics, and they have made this selection for me. Take a look at the recipe for grilled salt cod with olive oil and wine vinegar, a dish so simple it doesn't look worth the bother; but if your children enjoy fish and chips it's all of that in one mouthful without the grease or soggy batter (and with a green salad instead of chips).

Everyday dishes can still be special, and although we all need to keep budget in mind, families are important and we should treat ourselves sometimes. Individual preferences are a challenge, and children are no exception. My eldest daughter, Sadie, has been a vegetarian since the age of seven and is the worst possible advertisement for fish. She holds her nose whenever she walks into one of our shops or restaurants, muttering 'Yuk' under her breath – and there isn't even a smell! One day I'm going to take delight in sharing a plate of oysters with her as she grows from a determined sixteen-year-old into a fish-lover. (In fact she did her first shift at the Bath restaurant recently, so I'm getting somewhere!)

My children come to the fishmonger's with me, and my son, Ben, really loves it. He will eat plates of oysters, urchins and crabs, in fact, he enjoys everything. Isobel, aged one, is following in his footsteps. Take your children along and get them involved. I love it when I hear children saying to their parents, 'I'd like to try that' (or 'I'd love to eat you,' whispered, through funnelled hands, to a crab!). If you start with 'safe' things like a tuna steak or a piece of smoked haddock or a big bowl of hot garlicky mussels, it gives you the opportunity to slip in the odd oyster or spiky sea urchin. Or put a whole crab on the table with a few bits of newspaper for the rubbish, and a small hammer. They will love it. I can remember my grandmother keeping me quiet for hours like that!

Food is so important. If you really want your children to appreciate fish as a pleasure and as a help in sustaining good health, you must involve and encourage them as much as possible. A weekly cookery lesson is time well spent.

Braised Hake with Shellfish, Parsley and Peas

This is a nice simple stew which can be made on the stove top. It makes the best of hake, which is a splendid fish – its flesh is moist and creamy and the simple flavours of the shellfish, fresh peas and parsley really work with it.

At the fishmonger's 'Two hake steaks, cut from the middle of the fish, weighing about 160 grams each, and six clams and six mussels.' Small hake, which are sometimes called pins, can also be used – just cut off the heads and cook them whole. Cod, haddock, pollack and ling are good alternatives.

You will need (serves 2) 25 g butter — 1 small onion, finely chopped — 1 clove of garlic, finely chopped — 25 ml olive oil — 2 × 160 g hake steaks — 1 tablespoon plain flour — ½ a wineglass of white wine — 6 mussels — 6 clams — a good handful of fresh or frozen peas — a handful of fresh parsley, chopped — salt and freshly ground black pepper — a squeeze of lemon — all-i-oli to serve (see page 25)

To make Melt the butter in a heavy-bottomed pan with a lid, big enough to take all the ingredients. Soften the onions, then the garlic, and push to one side. Add the olive oil to the pan. Lightly dust the hake with flour and fry the steaks on each side until golden. Add the wine and allow it to reduce by half and thicken, then add the mussels, clams, peas and half the parsley. Cover the pan and cook over a gentle heat for 5–6 minutes until all the shellfish has opened. Discard any that stay closed. Remove the hake, making sure it is properly cooked, and put it into a serving dish. Stir the remaining parsley into the juices in the pan, adding a little water if more juice is needed. Season with salt, freshly ground black pepper and a squeeze of lemon and then spoon over the hake.

To serve A bowl of rich all-i-oli to spoon over the top and some of yesterday's bread lightly rubbed with a cut or roasted tomato is all you need with this.

Hake with Crisp Sweet Garlic and Good Olive Oil

The way you use certain ingredients can change the taste of a dish. When garlic is cut into really thin slices across the clove it can be fried until crisp, which gives it a sweetness and changes the flavour of the whole dish; this is how it is used here.

Some fried slices of hake, a bit of sliced garlic, some good olive oil, some parsley and lemon juice will remind you how good simple dishes with reliable ingredients can be.

At the fishmonger's 'Six steaks, 2.5 centimetres thick, preferably from the middle of the fish.' Hake are gutted from the middle of the fish to the head, and steaks taken from the back end will be solid, round chunks of meat. Those from the top half are still superb, but I prefer the look of the smaller rounder steaks from the back half of the fish. The choice is yours.

You will need (serves 2) olive oil — 6 hake steaks — sea salt and freshly ground black pepper — 2 cloves of garlic, very finely sliced — good extra virgin olive oil — juice of ½ a lemon — a handful of fresh flat-leaf parsley, finely chopped

---

To make Get a heavy-based frying pan really hot, then add just enough olive oil to fry the fish in. Season the steaks with a light sprinkling of sea salt and freshly ground black pepper. Lay the fish in the pan and fry for a minute or two, then add the garlic. Keep frying till the garlic is golden brown with a sweet flavour. Turn the fish after 3–4 minutes and cook it for 3 minutes on the other side. Make sure the garlic doesn't burn. Remove the fish from the pan to a serving dish.

With the pan off the heat, add a good splash of your finest extra virgin olive oil and a pinch of sea salt to the garlic and juices left in the pan. The residual heat of the pan will be sufficient to warm it all through; there is no need to put it back on the flame. Add a good squeeze of lemon juice, then the parsley, and give it all a good stir. You just know even before you dress the fish that it is going to taste good.

To serve Place the fish slightly overlapping on a serving dish and spoon the juices from the pan over the top. Boiled or mashed potatoes go well with this, or some fresh beans from the garden. One piece of fish per person makes a good starter, and for a few more people serve it family-style and let everyone help themselves.

Try this too ... Gurnard, pollack and small cod steaks and fillets of bream also work exceptionally well. Replace the parsley with rosemary, or add a few finely chopped salted anchovies, some ground cumin and a sprinkling of pine nuts to the pan before serving.

Crisp Fried Rock Salmon with Bubble and Squeak and Tartare Sauce

Rock salmon, huss or flake, as it is known depending on which part of the country you come from, is actually dogfish, but I think the other names suit it better. In the trade they are always skinned first and are sold as 'skinned dogs', looking like a long, white eel with an almost pinkish tinge. They are just about impossible to skin yourself and it takes a strong arm and experience to be able to do it. If I'm doing the ordering for one of the restaurants and I want to wind up the guys I order their dogfish and skate skin-on – they go mad!

Rock salmon has a delicious, soft, moist texture and I am amazed that we don't eat more of it. It's my mum's favourite. It's very English and it seems appropriate to serve it with bubble and squeak rather than chips, and a good, chunky tartare sauce packed with capers and pickles or a dollop of HP.

At the fishmonger's 'Four pieces of rock salmon fillet about 20 centimetres in length, from the top end of the fish.' The fish is thickest at the top end, just behind the head. Fresh rock salmon should have a pink tinge, and should have no smell at all. Fish a few days old will smell of ammonia, from the uric acid in the flesh. This also happens with shark and skate.

You will need (serves 4) 4 pieces of rock salmon fillet — sea salt and freshly ground black pepper — 3 tablespoons plain flour — 2 eggs, beaten — fresh white breadcrumbs (or use panko, Japanese breadcrumbs which are available in most supermarkets and oriental stores) — 1 small onion, finely chopped — vegetable oil — enough mashed potato for 4 — 250 g cooked sprouts or cabbage, roughly chopped — a small handful of fresh parsley, chopped — a splash of anchovy essence — tartare sauce to serve (see page 23) — lemon wedges to serve

---

To make Season the fish with a little salt and pepper. Dip it first in the flour, then the beaten egg, then the breadcrumbs, and put on a plate in the fridge until needed.

Gently fry the onion in a little oil until just golden. Put the mashed potato into a bowl with the cooked cabbage or sprouts and add the fried onion and a handful of chopped parsley. Add a splash of anchovy essence and a good turn of black pepper and mix well. Take a handful of the mixture, shape it into a ball about the size of a small orange, then flatten it and lightly dust it in flour. Make 4 of these. Fry them in a little oil until golden each side, then pop them into a medium oven while you cook the fish. Heat the oil in a deep-fat fryer to 190°C – if you are using a saucepan it should be no more than half full of oil, and a piece of bread should turn golden in 6–7 seconds when dropped in. Fry the fish in the oil for 4–5 minutes until golden, then drain on kitchen paper.

To serve Place a bubble and squeak cake in the middle of each plate. Spread tartare sauce over each one and sit a piece of rock salmon on top. Garnish with a lemon wedge and a sprig of parsley. Tomato ketchup, vinegar and extra salt are always asked for around my table.

Try this too . . . Add fresh garlic to the breadcrumbs. Warm hollandaise sauce can be used instead of tartare. Don't just stick to sprouts and cabbage in your bubble and squeak, any left-over vegetables will do.

Grilled Salt Cod with Olive Oil and Wine Vinegar

My friend Orlando in Portugal told me about his mother's recipe for salt cod. He said it was absolutely delicious – it was soaked, grilled over a fire, then drizzled with olive oil and vinegar. One day while I was putting this book together I had a bit of salt cod left over, and decided to try it. I grilled the fish on a grill plate, finished it in the oven for a few minutes, then drizzled it with olive oil and white wine vinegar. The smell was wonderful, and the flavour was even better – it tasted like the *best* fish and chips that I had ever had. The fish just broke away in big white flakes and I knew the kids were going to love it.

At the fishmonger's 'Four pieces of cod from the thick end, about 175 grams each.' I prefer the thick end of cod as the flakes are bigger and more succulent. If it is not available then smaller pieces will be fine. Allow time for salting and soaking when you decide to make this.

You will need (serves 4) 4 × 175 g pieces of cod — 800 g rock salt — good olive oil — white wine vinegar to taste

---

To make First salt and soak your cod (see page 36). When you have tasted a little corner of the flesh and decided that enough salt has been removed, heat a grill pan or plate on top of the stove for 5–10 minutes until it has reached maximum heat. Preheat the oven to 200°C/400°F/gas 6. Lightly brush the cod with olive oil and lay it flesh-side down on the grill plate for 4 minutes. Turn it over and continue to cook for another 2–3 minutes, then finish in the preheated oven for a couple of extra minutes. Put on to serving plates and drizzle with good olive oil and vinegar to your taste.

To serve Fresh peas with mint, creamy mashed potato, and a dollop of tartare sauce or all-i-oli are good with this. Even something as simple as a bowl of gherkins will do, but the possibilities are endless – think of fish and chips.

Roasted Cod with Fennel, Mustard, Ginger and Chicory Salad

Once I've chosen a piece of fish to cook the next question is always what am I going to eat it with, and while there is nothing wrong with simply grilled or roasted fish with olive oil, sea salt and lemon juice – I shout about how good it is all the time – I also like to think about other flavours that I enjoy and try to combine them in a way that will make an interesting accompaniment or garnish. Just looking at good colourful produce in your greengrocer's can inspire you.

Fennel is one of my favourite vegetables, whether it is braised, roasted or raw in a salad. At first, I thought chicory was a bit bitter, but I have really grown to like it a lot. This ginger and mustard dressing helped.

At the fishmonger's 'Four 160 gram pieces of cod fillet from the thick end.' If cod isn't available, use hake, haddock, pollack . . . in fact I can't think of a fish that wouldn't work well with this.

You will need (serves 4) 2.5 cm fresh root ginger, peeled and very finely chopped — 2 teaspoons sugar — 1 large fennel bulb — 1 head of chicory — 4 spring onions — 1 egg yolk — a splash of white wine vinegar — 1 teaspoon grain mustard — 100 ml groundnut, vegetable or any other neutral-flavoured oil — sea salt and freshly ground black pepper — 4 × 160 g cod fillets — optional: lemon juice

---

To make First make the ginger syrup by putting the ginger and sugar into a saucepan with 75 ml of water. Bring it gently to the boil until all the sugar has dissolved. Taste to see whether the ginger is prominent – if not, add a little more. It will taste quite sweet, but remember that is going to be balanced with the white wine vinegar and mustard. The syrup can be made in advance and stored in the fridge.

Preheat the oven to its maximum temperature. Remove the tougher outer leaves from the fennel bulb, and the tough stalks. If there are lots of feathery fronds on the top pick these off to use in the salad. Slice the bulb as thinly as you can. Take the outer leaves from the chicory, then pull off about 2 leaves per person and trim about 1 cm off the bottom of each one. Cut the spring onions into juliennes (very fine strips, like you get with Chinese crispy duck).

To make the dressing, put the egg yolk, vinegar and mustard into a bowl and whisk together. Still whisking, add a steady stream of oil until you have a thin emulsion. Then add the ginger syrup and pieces of ginger, a teaspoon at a time, until there is a balance between the harshness of the vinegar and mustard and the sweet syrup. You will know when it is right. Lastly, season with salt and freshly ground black pepper.

Add some vegetable oil to a hot pan and fry the cod fillets, skin side down, for 4–5 minutes until the skin is crisp. Turn the cod over, then put the whole pan (or transfer to a roasting tray) into the preheated oven and cook for a further 6 or 7 minutes. While the fish is in the oven toss the fennel, chicory and spring onions lightly in the dressing and place 2 chicory leaves in the middle of each plate with a handful of the fennel and spring onions on top. Lay each piece of fish on top. Sprinkle with sea salt and a squeeze of lemon if you like.

Try this too . . . For an extra bit of colour try using a mixture of red and green chicory, or if chicory is not available use quarters of sweet little gem lettuces instead.

Deep-fried Smoked Haddock with Lime, Cucumber and Mint Salad

Smoked haddock is normally grilled or poached, but it's delicious deep-fried in a light batter. A pinch of curry powder or a teaspoon of curry paste goes a long way with smoked haddock. I like to add it to the hollandaise sauce when I make haddock and poached eggs. I tried adding a pinch to this batter mixture and it was really good – try it.

At the fishmonger's 'Two pieces of smoked haddock, skinned, 150 grams in weight each.' Look for haddock that has been naturally smoked, not dyed, it will taste better. If it is not available then ask for cod or other smoked white fish.

You will need (serves 2) 4 tablespoons cornflour — 6 tablespoons self-raising flour — 1 teaspoon curry powder or paste — a pinch of salt — a few glugs of beer (drink the rest!) — ice-cold sparkling mineral water — 2 × 150 g pieces of smoked haddock — lime wedges to serve — lime, cucumber and mint salad (see page 187)

To make Mix the flours with the curry powder and salt, add the beer, then gradually whisk in the mineral water until you have a batter the consistency of double cream. If using curry paste, stir it in now. Dip the smoked haddock into this mixture and deep fry at 190°C for 4–5 minutes until crisp and golden.

To serve Serve with lime wedges and the lime, cucumber and mint salad.

Grilled Sardine and Tomato Paste

This is fabulous in sandwiches with fresh cucumber, eaten as part of your picnic on the way down to the beach. It is better than anything you will get out of a jar. Spread it on toast and pop it under the grill with a few slices of tomato to make a great quick supper when you are in a hurry.

At the fishmonger's 'Three large sardines, filleted.' You can use small herrings and small mackerel, but if you do, ask your fishmonger to take the pinbones out for you. They won't bother you in a sardine as they are so small but in a mackerel they will be slightly larger.

You will need (makes about 300 g) 3 large sardines, filleted — a handful of fresh white breadcrumbs — 1 heaped tablespoon salted capers, rinsed — 1 shallot, finely diced — 1 tablespoon tomato purée — 1 ripe tomato — a few splashes of Worcestershire Sauce — 4–5 drops of Tabasco — salt and freshly ground black pepper — 100 ml olive oil — 75 g soft butter

---

To make Grill the sardines on a hot grill plate, skin side down, until nicely charred. Turn them over and cook for a further 1–2 minutes, then allow them to cool. Put them into a food processor with all the other ingredients except the olive oil and butter and blitz to a smooth paste. Gently drizzle in the olive oil and fold in the softened butter. Chill for an hour before using.

To serve I don't think that this can be beaten spread on to freshly baked bread and topped with thin slices of cucumber or radish.

Try this too ... You could stir this into cooked spaghetti with lemon juice, olive oil, pine nuts, raisins and chopped fennel. If you don't fancy sardines, try making it with a small piece of grilled tuna and adding a touch of chilli or oregano.

Fish as good as this can simply be filleted and marinated in white wine vinegar with chopped garlic for 20 minutes. then drain them and serve them with a drizzle of olive oil and a sprinkle of chopped parsley.

Fish Fingers and Mayonnaise

These are what they are, fingers of fresh fish with a crispy coating and deep-fried. What I like about my fish fingers is that I know what is in them. Fish.

At the fishmonger's 'Four 25 gram pieces of cod, cut across the fillet from the tail end and skinned.' You could buy one tail end piece of cod (which will have no bones) and cut this into fingers yourself. I've suggested cod, but you can also use pollack, haddock and large whiting (which never seem to get any good press, but believe me they are delicious).

You will need (serves 2 children) 2 tablespoons cornflour — 2 tablespoons plain flour — a pinch of salt — ice-cold sparkling mineral water — a handful of fresh, fine breadcrumbs — 4 × 25 g pieces of cod or other white fish — mayonnaise or seafood cocktail sauce (see pages 23 and 25, though I suspect tomato ketchup will win every time)

To make Mix the flours with the salt and whisk in enough mineral water to make a batter the consistency of double cream. Stir in the breadcrumbs, and a little more water if needed. Dip the fish fingers in the batter and deep fry for 3–4 minutes until crisp and golden. They can be shallow fried in hot oil too.

To serve Peas and mashed potato! Plus ketchup or whatever sauce you choose.

Poached Plaice with Cider and Onions

Plaice are pretty to look at. Their spots should look as if they have been airbrushed on and be as vibrant and bright as the colours you find in a surf shop. During August and September we get the most magnificent fish – they can weigh up to 3 kilos, which means they are big enough to cut into steaks, like small turbot and brill. When they are as big as that the flesh is even more moist and creamier than smaller fish. I don't think plaice can be likened to anything else. Small children love this because they think they are getting their first taste of cider!

At the fishmonger's 'Two fillets of plaice, from a fish weighing about 600–700 grams.' Flat fish will only give you about 50 per cent yield, so you will end up with two portions weighing between 150 and 175 grams. The fillet from the top of the fish will always be thicker than that from the bottom. If your fishmonger only has large fish, ask for the top fillet only and cut it in two straight down the middle.

You will need (serves 2) 25 g butter — a glug of olive oil — 1 large onion, thinly sliced — 2 cloves of garlic, crushed — 500 ml good-quality dry cider — 2 bay leaves — 2 sprigs of fresh thyme — 2 × 150–175 g plaice fillets — a small handful of fresh parsley, finely chopped — salt and freshly ground black pepper

To make Melt the butter in a heavy-bottomed pan and add the olive oil. Add the onions and cook slowly for 10–15 minutes so that they gently brown and melt but do not fry. Add the garlic, cider, bay leaves and thyme and simmer for 5–6 minutes. Add the fish and, with the liquid barely simmering, allow it to poach for 6–7 minutes. Lift the fish fillets out and place them on a serving plate. Add the parsley to the pan, turn the heat up and reduce the liquid by a third. Season to taste.

To serve Place a pile of onions on top of each piece of fish and spoon the remaining juices around. Alternatively, put the fish back into the pan and take the whole thing to the table. Creamy mashed potato, haricot beans dressed with thyme and olive oil, or buttered cabbage with just a bit of shredded smoked bacon are great with this.

Try this too ... When the onions have melted, add some cooked butter beans or haricot beans, or some chopped fennel, to make more of a stew. Skate is excellent cooked the same way.

Steamed Mussels with Wine and Parsley Leaf

This is one of the most simple and reliable recipes for cooking mussels. It is always enjoyable and the kids love it.

At the fishmonger's Allow 600 grams of mussels per person as a main course and 300 grams as a starter. The usual rules for buying mussels apply: they should be closed when you buy them and open when you cook them.

You will need 2 cloves of garlic, fincly chopped — 1 shallot, finely chopped — a glug of olive oil — 25 g butter — 1 wineglass of dry white wine — 600 g mussels per person — a handful of fresh parsley leaves, chopped

To make Put the olive oil and butter into a large pan and add the garlic and shallot. Cook gently until softened. Do not allow them to brown. Add the wine, boil for a minute and then add the mussels. Replace the lid and cook, giving the pan a shake from time to time. The mussels are ready when they have opened – discard any that don't. Spoon the mussels into a serving bowl, then stir the parsley into the juices in the pan and pour over the mussels.

Grilled Mussels Stuffed with Pancetta, Garlic and Green Pepper

There is lots of flavour in these lovely stuffed mussels. They are perfect before dinner with drinks. Serve them on the biggest plate you've got and stack them high.

At the fishmonger's 'A kilo of mussels.' Buy the largest ones you can find – they will be easier to stuff, grill and eat. The small rope-grown variety are more fiddly but still worth buying. Remember the basic rule: they should be closed when you buy them, open when you've cooked them.

You will need (serves 2) 1 kg mussels — a splash of white wine — 25 g butter — 1 shallot, finely chopped — 1 clove of garlic, finely chopped — ½ a green pepper, deseeded and finely chopped — 50 g pancetta or smoked bacon, minced — 3 plum tomatoes, roughly chopped — a few drops of Tabasco — a pinch of cayenne pepper — a handful of fresh white breadcrumbs — a small handful of fresh parsley, chopped — 1 lemon

---

To make Clean the mussels by washing them under cold running water and removing the beards with a gentle tug. Put them with the wine into a pan with a tight-fitting lid and steam them open. Throw away any that stay closed. When they are cool enough to handle, remove the meat, roughly chop and set aside, reserving the cooking liquid. Snap apart the two shells of each mussel, and lay out on a roasting tray which will fit under the grill. Some crumpled tinfoil on the grill tray will help keep the mussels from tipping over.

Melt the butter in a pan and gently sweat the shallot, garlic and green pepper until softened. Add the pancetta and cook for a further 3–4 minutes, then add the tomatoes. Pour in the reserved mussel juice, add the Tabasco and cayenne, and continue to cook until only ½ a wineglass of liquid is left. Add the breadcrumbs, the chopped mussel meat and the parsley. The mixture should be loose and buttery. Place a spoonful in each mussel shell and pop under the grill for a minute or two until crisp.

Finish with a squeeze of lemon on each one before serving.

To serve This is a great dish for nibbling while chatting, with a few cold Belgian beers. Fantastic finger food.

Try this too ... Use large clams such as amandes, or razor clams, and make a stuffing with chopped ginger, garlic, lemon grass, lime leaves, chilli and breadcrumbs, just moistened with coconut milk. Sprinkle with chopped coriander and lime juice before serving.

Grilled Queen Scallops with Anchovy, Roasted Garlic and Mint

Queen scallops are the small ones that will fit into the palm of your hand; their meat is delicious and can be cooked in the same way as the more common, and larger, king scallop.

Mint works well with strong flavours like anchovy and the sweetness of roasted garlic. A pile of these is great for dinner.

At the fishmonger's 'Twelve queen scallops in the half shell.' If you can't get the scallop shells, fry the scallops and serve them on croûtons.

You will need (serves 2) 2 cloves of garlic — olive oil — a small handful of fresh mint leaves — 3 anchovy fillets — sea salt — 2 egg yolks — 75 g unsalted butter, melted — a pinch of cayenne pepper — lemon juice — 12 queen scallops in the shell

To make Put the garlic into a small roasting tray with a little olive oil and roast in the top of the oven at about 170°C/325°F/gas 3 for about 20 minutes until it is soft. Squeeze the garlic out of the skins into a pestle and mortar, add the mint, anchovies and some sea salt, and work to a smooth paste. It will smell great. Put the egg yolks into a heatproof glass bowl. Hold on to the edge of it with a towel, add a tablespoon of cold water, and keep whisking the yolks while you hold the bowl carefully hovering 12–15 cm above the flame on the stove top. You want to cook the eggs until they have a double-cream consistency – too much heat and they will end up as scrambled eggs, so don't put the bowl too near. Gradually add the melted butter in a thin stream, whisking as if making mayonnaise. The butter and eggs will emulsify and give you a thick buttery sauce. You have just made hollandaise. Stir in the garlic paste and add cayenne and lemon juice to taste.

Lay the scallops, in their shells, on a roasting tray, sprinkle lightly with sea salt and brush each one with just a little butter. Place under a hot grill for 2–3 minutes (no longer, as they can dry very quickly). Place a tablespoon of the sauce on each one and return to the hot grill until the sauce has lightly browned.

To serve I like to put a few handfuls of sea salt on to a plate to hold the scallops in place and sit them on top.

Try this too ... Melt some good garlic butter (see page 28) and stir in a handful of fresh white breadcrumbs. Spread on the raw scallops in the roasting tray and grill until the breadcrumbs have just crisped and the scallops are just cooked. Or try topping them with the parsley, garlic, hazelnut and salted anchovy pesto on page 22, or the parsley, garlic and hazelnut sauce used in the razor clam dish on page 132.

Hot Smoked Salmon Sandwich

I'm a bit of a traditionalist when it comes to smoked salmon. For me, the only way to serve it is thinly sliced by hand and laid over a nice large white plate, seasoned with just black pepper and lemon. Here, however, is a fun way to serve a smoked salmon sandwich that makes a great lunchtime snack for children.

You will need (serves 2) 4 slices of medium-cut white bread, crusts removed — 100 ml thick béchamel sauce (you can buy perfectly good ready-made ones or see page 20) — 100 g sliced smoked salmon — 1 tablespoon chopped fresh dill — freshly ground black pepper — a squeeze of lemon juice — a splash of milk — 2 eggs, beaten — butter for frying

To make Spread each slice of bread with the béchamel sauce, cover with smoked salmon, and sprinkle with dill, a few turns of black pepper and a few drops of lemon juice. Make 2 sandwiches and cut into 4 triangles. Mix the milk and beaten egg together, dip the sandwiches into this mixture and fry on either side in the butter until crisp and golden.

Tempura Prawns with Roasted Salt and Pepper

Tempura batter is light and crisp and is ideal for small nuggets of seafood like prawns, scallops and squid. It is easy to make and has so many uses. Dip oysters into it and fry them, or try small mussels and clams and experiment with different flavoured dipping sauces. Try lime juice, lemon grass, ginger, coriander, chilli and sugar with just a dash of fish sauce and cold water, or try the chilli jam on page 26. This roasted salt and pepper dip is easy and particularly good.

At the fishmonger's 'Two dozen raw prawns, about 16/20 size.' See page 84 for a note about prawn sizing. If prawns are unavailable, try any of the suggestions above.

You will need (serves 4) 24 raw prawns — 4 tablespoons plain flour — 4 tablespoons cornflour — a small bottle of sparkling mineral water, straight from the fridge — 1 tablespoon ground salt — 1 tablespoon Sichuan peppercorns — 1 tablespoon black peppercorns

---

To make Prepare the prawns by removing the heads and peeling off the shells, leaving the last segment of the shell and tail intact as these go crispy, are packed with flavour and are delicious to eat. They also make good grips to pick up the prawns with. Remove any dark veins running down the prawns. To make the batter, mix the two flours together well, then whisk in the cold sparkling water in a steady stream until the batter is the texture of double cream.

To make the dip, put the salt and the Sichuan and black peppercorns into a small frying pan and toast gently while shaking the pan. There will be a wonderful aroma. Place the roasted spices in a pestle and mortar or a spice grinder and grind until fine. Heat vegetable oil in a deep-fryer to 190°C, making sure you use clean oil. (You can use a saucepan half full of oil and heat it until a cube of bread turns golden in 6–7 seconds when dropped in.) Give the batter a final stir, hold each prawn by the tail, dip it in the batter, and drop it into the oil. Cook 3–4 at a time – if you add more the oil will cool down and the batter will become soggy. They will take 3–4 minutes to cook. The batter may not turn golden, especially when fresh, clean oil is used; instead it will be crisp, firm and white. I always give the basket a shake as I add each prawn, to stop it sinking to the bottom and knotting itself to the basket. Lift out the prawns when cooked and drain on kitchen paper.

To serve Lay out 4 plates and place a napkin on each. Put the salt and pepper dip into 4 small dipping bowls, espresso cups, egg cups, or just in a pile on the edge of the plate. Put some prawns on top of each napkin. (If you wish, you can garnish with parsley and a small wedge of lime.)

Salt Baked Prawns

Cooking fish in salt creates an oven within the oven and the flavours are really sealed in. It works just as well with shellfish too, as their flesh is protected by their shell. It is really easy. You just cover them in salt and bake them in the oven, then dig them out and serve (or do it at the table).

At the fishmonger's 'Two dozen 16/20 size raw prawns.' Langoustines or smaller prawns are a good alternative, but they must be raw.

You will need (serves 4) 1 kg rock salt — 24 raw prawns — 6 whole cloves of garlic, skin left on — 6 sprigs of fresh thyme — olive oil — lemon wedges, to serve

To make Preheat the oven to its maximum temperature. Sprinkle a thin layer of rock salt into a roasting dish. Lay the prawns and garlic on top. Sprinkle over the sprigs of thyme and completely cover with the remaining rock salt. Sprinkle a little water over the top and bake in the preheated oven for 10–12 minutes. Remove from the oven, break open the salt crust and serve the prawns with a little olive oil, the roasted garlic cloves and a few chunks of lemon.

The Best Scampi ... Ever

I really enjoy a good bowl of fried scampi but I can't get to grips with the processed nature of it. Scampi are actually langoustines or Dublin Bay prawns, and manufacturers produce what is called 'whole-tail' or, even worse, 're-formed' scampi, made from broken and badly damaged fish. This is not my kind of food. There is, however, nothing like a fresh plump langoustine tail coated in light breadcrumbs, deep fried and then dunked in a good well-made tartare sauce. It is always best to use the biggest langoustines you can find – they will come at a price, but I can assure you they are worth every penny.

At the fishmonger's 'A dozen large, live langoustines.' Live langoustines will always be the best (see page 72. They can be anything up to 250–300 grams each in weight, but the most likely size you will see will be between 60 and 80 grams.

You will need (serves 2, or 4 if you've managed to buy extra large langoustines)
12 langoustines — a pinch of sea salt — a handful of plain flour — 2 eggs, beaten —
a handful of fresh, white breadcrumbs (I use Japanese crumbs called panko, which are available
in most supermarkets and oriental stores) — vegetable oil for deep-frying — tartare sauce
(see page 23) or other dipping sauce (see below)

To make First kill your langoustines (as you would a lobster; see page 54). Twist the heads off the langoustines, carefully break open the shell and remove the tail meat. Sprinkle them with a little sea salt, then dip them one by one first in the flour, then the beaten egg, and last of all the breadcrumbs. When they are all done, heat oil in a deep-fryer to 180°C (or use a saucepan half full of vegetable oil and heat it until a cube of bread turns golden in 6–7 seconds when dropped into the hot fat). Fry the scampi in the hot oil, 3 or 4 at a time, for 2–3 minutes until golden, then drain on kitchen paper or a clean towel.

To serve I like to serve this on one plate for people to share. Put a napkin on the plate and pile the scampi on top. On the table put a small bowl of tartare sauce, mayonnaise with a good added squeeze of lemon or all-i-oli. Or make a seafood sauce with mayonnaise, Tabasco, tomato ketchup, Worcestershire Sauce, a splash of whisky and just a squeeze of lemon.

Try this too ... If langoustines are not available try fresh prawns, prepared in exactly the same way, or slices of monkfish, or scallops.

Easy Food for Guests

I love having friends home to eat with us. When something special arrives in the shop I can't resist picking up the phone straight away and inviting a few people to join us for supper. I wouldn't be doing this if fish cookery were difficult. I bet most people who cook for 2 or more wouldn't consider fish as an option, although they would probably like to. I can tell you from experience that a couple of kilos of mussels, a handful of herbs and some spaghetti will take about 15 minutes from start to finish and can be served from one bowl at the table, saving you a lot of work. Not only that, but you can probably make enough for 5–6 people for under a tenner. Fish is perfect for these occasions.

Home kitchens aren't like those in a restaurant – there are no hot lamps, big wide spaces, or professionals to help you. So I serve everything family-style: I love to have the table brimming with salads, the cold accompaniments, the bread and wine and warm plates ready in people's places, so that all that remains is to bring on the hot dish. Anticipation gets everyone chatting, and it is great to see their faces when you plonk a whole roasted turbot in front of them. You will feel proud and appreciated, and they will feel special too.

Keep it really simple: roast a whole fish and serve it with just a drizzle of oil, a sprinkle of sea salt and a bowl of cut lemons. For bass, bream, mullet and any other round fish, allow about 275 g of whole fish per person. For flat fish, like lemon sole or turbot and brill, allow 350 g. Whack the oven up to its highest setting for 5–10 minutes before you start cooking. Place the fish on a roasting tray, sprinkle it with salt, a few glugs of olive oil and maybe some thyme or rosemary, and roast it in the oven for 15–20 minutes (for a fish weighing about 500 g). For larger fish, just keep checking regularly after this time until the flesh is cooked – a fish weighing a kilo doesn't need double the time. Keep checking until the flesh is milky white, moist and juicy. Cooking fish for a big table is easy, and everything in this section is ideal for big get-togethers.

Crisp Fried Marinated Whitebait with Parsley and Olive Oil

Whitebait are small fish fry and are caught only at certain times of the year. They are not commercially fished in any great quantity in the UK any more. Last year I went down to the river Fowey in Cornwall to see Dave, the chap who cultivates mussels and oysters for us. He was showing me some live sand eels which he nets to use as bait when he goes bass fishing and I asked him if he knew how good these things were to eat. The look and reply that I got back meant that he didn't! I tried to talk him into starting to fish for them, but he didn't fancy it. Then he said that next year he would put out a few nets to catch the local whitebait. I couldn't believe it. I had never been anywhere where it was possible to catch it fresh. Right in front of me was a place that he said would be teeming with it during the season. Nobody fishes for it because nobody really wants it. It's unbelievable.

Whitebait are mainly sold frozen and nowadays you more often see them coated in breadcrumbs. They look huge, and you just know that it is all breadcrumb and no fish. Even when you buy them without that coating they are usually just deep-fried and tossed with cayenne pepper. There is nothing wrong with that and I love it, but try this – it's a bit different.

At the fishmonger's 'A bag of frozen whitebait!' If you are lucky enough to live somewhere where fresh whitebait is common, allow about 200 grams per person.

You will need 200 g whitebait per person — sea salt and freshly ground black pepper — plain flour — 150 ml cider vinegar — 1 tablespoon caster sugar — 2 onions, thinly sliced — 1 small carrot, finely chopped — 2 cloves of garlic, chopped — ½ a stick of celery, finely chopped — olive oil — 1 bay leaf — a good handful of fresh flat-leaf parsley, chopped

---

To make Dredge the whitebait in seasoned flour and deep-fry for 3–4 minutes until crisp. Drain and set aside. Gently warm the vinegar and sugar until the sugar has dissolved and the mixture is slightly sweet, then leave to cool.

Gently fry the onions, carrot, garlic and celery in a little olive oil until golden. Add the vinegar and sugar mix and the bay leaf. Continue to cook for 2–3 minutes, then set aside to cool. Add plenty of chopped parsley. Arrange the whitebait in a serving dish in a thin layer and spoon the marinade over the top. Finish with crunchy sea salt and plenty of freshly ground black pepper.

Fritto Misto

Fried fish with nothing more than some lemon juice and a little oil and chopped parsley. 'Fritto misto' simply means 'mixed fried', and any fish can be included as long as it really is at its best. My choices are squid, prawns cooked in their shells, a small fillet of sea bass or bream and small red mullet, my favourite fish, weighing around 100 g each. If you like shellfish, then lightly steam some mussels, clams or razor clams, remove them from their shells and fry them with the other fish.

At the fishmonger's Just buy a selection of small whole fish, and fillets or steaks of the freshest fish on the counter. Include a bit of shellfish too. The more variety of fish that you are able to buy the more interesting your fritto misto will be, but even if only two or three species are available you will still enjoy the simplicity of this recipe. Allow about 300–400 grams of fish per person. If you are buying fillets, allow around 175 grams. To save yourself a job, ask the fishmonger to scale and gut all of the fish, but leave the heads and tails on unless you really would prefer not to.

You will need (per person) a pinch of sea salt — 300–400 g mixed fish (see above) — 250 ml milk — a couple of handfuls of good strong white flour — vegetable oil — 2 lemons, cut into quarters — a couple of tablespoons of chopped parsley

---

To make Sprinkle a little sea salt over the prepared fish, then dip the fish one at a time into the milk and then into the flour, shaking them to remove any excess flour. Cover the base of a large, wide frying pan with about 1 centimetre of vegetable oil and heat to around 150–160°C, or until a cube of bread turns golden in 6–7 seconds when thrown into the oil. Fry each piece of fish until crisp and golden on each side. If you have any larger pieces of fish, remove them from the pan, place them on a roasting dish and finish the cooking in the oven, preheated to its maximum. But you will not need to do this if you select smaller fish. Drain on kitchen paper before serving.

To serve Lay the fish in a single layer on a white plate, sprinkle with parsley, and add a squeeze of lemon juice and maybe a drizzle of good olive oil.

Cod Steaks with Potato Gnocchi, Chilli and Rich Tomato Sauce

I am a big fan of gnocchi. I often buy a pack of ready-made ones from my local Italian deli, though if I have the time I like to chill out and make my own. These gnocchi with tomato and chilli sauce can be served with just about any fish, but I like them with cod.

At the fishmonger's 'Four cod steaks, about 165 grams each.' If you can't get cod use steaks of hake cut from the middle of the fish, or small monkfish fillets.

You will need (serves 4) 1 small onion, finely chopped — 1 clove of garlic, finely chopped — olive oil — 2 tablespoons red wine — 1 tablespoon balsamic vinegar — 200 ml tomato passata — 1 fresh tomato, roughly chopped — 1 mild fresh red chilli, finely chopped — vegetable oil — 4 × 165 g cod steaks — sea salt and freshly ground black pepper — 200 g ready-prepared potato gnocchi — a handful of fresh parsley, chopped — lemon juice

---

To make First make the tomato sauce. Gently fry the onions and garlic in a few tablespoons of olive oil for about 20 minutes until lightly golden and melted. Add the red wine and allow to boil until almost nothing is left, then do the same with the balsamic vinegar. Add the passata, tomato and chilli, then add a little water and continue to cook until the tomato is melted and you have a rich sauce. Preheat the oven to its maximum temperature. Heat some vegetable oil in a frying pan suitable for the oven. Sprinkle the cod with sea salt and fry until golden on the flesh side. Then place the whole pan in the preheated oven for 4–5 minutes to finish the cooking.

Cook the gnocchi in plenty of boiling salted water until they float to the surface. Drain them, then stir them into the sauce. Add some chopped parsley and some lemon juice. Remove the cod from the oven.

To serve Place a few tablespoons of the gnocchi and sauce in each bowl. Peel the skin off the cod, then sit it on top and sprinkle over some sea salt and some lemon juice. A big dish of peas with prosciutto (see page 180) is a fabulous accompaniment.

Try this too ... Warm 200 ml of béchamel sauce (see page 20, or use ready-made sauce from a carton) and stir in lots of freshly ground black pepper and parsley. Stir the cooked gnocchi into this, finish with lemon juice and serve with the cod on top.

Haddock with Creamed Leeks, Runner Beans and Chervil

Creamed leeks are particularly delicious – I pinched the recipe off Matthew Prowse, the head chef in our Bristol restaurant. He serves them with roasted turbot. I think they are delicious enough to serve with anything and I can't resist picking at them when I go into his kitchen (he doesn't put them on the menu when he knows I'm coming). I've made them even better now, though, by adding the runner beans and chervil!

At the fishmonger's 'Four 75 gram pieces of haddock fillet from the thick end.' If haddock is not available, try salmon, hake, a nice chunk of brill or scallops.

You will need (serves 4) 2 medium leeks — 50 g runner beans — 200 ml double cream — sea salt and freshly ground black pepper — 1 teaspoon English mustard — optional: 1 teaspoon hazelnut oil — vegetable oil — 4 × 75 g haddock fillets — a small handful of fresh chervil, chopped

To make Remove the roots from the leeks and cut off the tops. Split the leeks in half and chop as finely as possible, then wash to remove any mud or dirt.

Prepare the runner beans using a bean slicer or just remove the strings from the side and chop them into fine slices on a slant across the bean. Place the leeks and beans into an empty saucepan, stir them together and cover. Place them over a gentle heat, checking every minute or so and giving them a stir – you will be surprised how much liquid will come out of the leeks, and they won't burn. Continue to stir until the leeks and runner beans have softened, which will take 7 or 8 minutes. Strain the liquid off and return the leeks and beans to the pan with the cream, a pinch of salt, a teaspoon of mustard and the hazelnut oil (if you like). Add some freshly ground black pepper (I like lots), and continue to cook for a few more minutes. You can cook these vegetables in advance – they are easy to reheat.

Preheat the oven to its maximum temperature. Add some vegetable oil to a hot frying pan. Season the fish with a little sea salt and fry flesh side down until golden for 5–6 minutes, then put the pan (or transfer the fillets to a roasting tray) into the preheated oven for a further 3–4 minutes.

To serve Add the chervil to the leeks, place a spoonful in the middle of each plate and place the fish on top.

Try this too . . . If runner beans aren't available, try using chopped fine green beans or thin slices of carrot. If you don't like the taste of chervil, simply leave it out or use parsley instead. Replace the mustard with curry powder, add a few fresh peas and serve it with grilled or poached smoked haddock.

Soused Aromatic Mackerel with Onions, Garlic, Mint and Creamy Mashed Potato

I remember the word 'soused' from when my grandmother was alive; she would talk about soused this and that but I never knew what she meant. When fish is soused it means it is baked in vinegar and aromatics. It can be served cold – the flesh of the fish is wonderfully moist and flavoured and makes a quick summertime lunch – or hot with creamy mashed potato and maybe a bit of buttered cabbage on the side.

At the fishmonger's 'Two mackerel, filleted.' When buying mackerel look for bright vibrant colours: petrol greens, shades of purple and bright silver should hit you straight away. After a day or so the colour is lost and only shades of black or grey can be seen. Mackerel is one of those fish that needs to be eaten as fresh as possible and I'm afraid there isn't a compromise. You can also use sardine fillets, gurnard, red or grey mullet and even tuna.

You will need (serves 2 as a main course or 4 as a starter) 2 pieces of star anise
— ½ teaspoon coriander seeds — ½ teaspoon mustard seeds — 4–5 allspice berries —
½ teaspoon black peppercorns — 6 cloves — a pinch of mace — 2 small dried chillies
— 2.5 cm fresh root ginger, peeled and chopped — 2 bay leaves —
150 ml white wine vinegar — 50 ml water — 50 ml dry white wine — 4 level tablespoons sugar
— 3 cloves of garlic, finely sliced — 1 small onion, finely sliced — 2 mackerel, filleted —
a pinch of salt — a handful of fresh mint, chopped

To make Preheat the oven to 180°C/350°F/gas 4. Put all the dried spices and the ginger (but not the bay leaves) into a pestle and mortar. Give them a quick bash to break the seeds and berries open, then place in a saucepan with the bay leaves, vinegar, water, wine and sugar. Bring to the boil and simmer for 10 minutes. Strain and discard the spices, then add the sliced garlic and onions, cover and cook gently for a further 10 minutes until the onions have softened. Place the fish flesh-side down in a casserole dish, sprinkle with a little salt and pour the spiced liquid over the top. The fish should be just covered; top it up with a little water if necessary. Cover the dish and bake in the preheated oven for 20 minutes. Remove from the oven, sprinkle with the mint and serve.

To serve Place 1 mackerel fillet on each plate if serving as a starter, 2 for a main course. Make sure everybody gets a pile of the onions and garlic and plenty of fresh mint and spoon a little of the juice over the top. Serve with buttery mashed potatoes and, if you like, a little buttered cabbage with maybe a pinch of caraway added.

Try this too … Use gooseberry vinegar (see page 35) instead of white wine vinegar and add a few crushed fresh gooseberries while the fish is cooking in the oven. If this tastes a little sharp, balance it with sugar and remember that the fresh mint will give the dish a lift too.

Rock Salmon Cooked as Osso Bucco

Osso bucco is an Italian veal dish. The flavours in it include wine, lemon, garlic and parsley, which are flavours that are good with fish too. I like braising fish, and steaks of rock salmon remind me a little bit of osso bucco – I think that is what started me off on this one.

At the fishmonger's 'Twelve steaks of rock salmon, about 8 centimetres long.' See page 92 for how to recognize fresh rock salmon. If rock salmon is not available you can use monkfish steaks or gurnard fillets the same way.

You will need (serves 4) 3 large plump cloves of garlic, finely chopped — a good handful of fresh flat-leaf parsley, finely chopped — olive oil — 1 shallot, finely chopped — 4 plum tomatoes, roughly chopped — 1 tablespoon tomato purée — 1 tablespoon anchovy paste — 1 large wineglass of dry white wine — 12 rock salmon steaks — zest of 1 lemon — sea salt and freshly ground black pepper — lemon wedges to garnish

To make Preheat the oven to 170°C/325°F/gas 3. Mix together the garlic and parsley. Pour some olive oil into a casserole dish large enough to take all of the pieces of fish standing upright, and gently sweat the shallot until golden. Add the tomatoes, tomato purée and anchovy paste and cook for a further minute. Add the wine and stir well. Boil for a few minutes to take the alcohol off the wine, then add half the garlic and parsley. Add the fish steaks to the pan, standing upright, put the lid on the casserole, and transfer it to the preheated oven for 40 minutes. Check it half-way through – if it needs more moisture, add a glass of water.

Remove from the oven and put 3 pieces of fish on each plate. Put the casserole back on to a medium heat and add the lemon zest and the remaining parsley and garlic to the juices in the pan. Simmer for 2–3 minutes, season with sea salt and freshly ground black pepper, then spoon the juices over the fish.

To serve This makes a lovely dinner party dish served on individual plates garnished with lemon wedges. It's good for everyday eating too, served family-style in one dish. A good herb or plain creamy risotto makes a wonderful accompaniment.

Try this too ... To make the dish more of a stew, add an extra $1/2$ wineglass of water at the beginning, a sprig of fresh thyme and a tin of borlotti or butter beans.

Grilled Tuna with Baked Aubergines, Tomato, Cumin and Mozzarella

Recently I managed to buy the freshest mozzarella that I have ever tasted. The experience was so good. I broke it like an egg and the middle just oozed. It was like nothing else that I have had before.

I baked aubergines and tomatoes with a bit of cumin, an onion and lots of garlic in small individual dishes, similar to ramekins but large enough to hold a serving for one, and served them alongside a simple grilled piece of tuna with nothing more than sea salt, lemon and good olive oil. I love the way the tomato sauce bubbles over the sides of the little dishes and the mozzarella melts over the top. Try it.

At the fishmonger's 'Four tuna steaks, weighing 175 grams each.' Try to get steaks cut from the thicker end of the loin, as they are a better shape and less sinewy than those from the tail end. If you can't get tuna you can use swordfish or marlin.

You will need (serves 4) 2 aubergines, cut into thin rounds — sea salt — olive oil — 1 onion, finely chopped — 3 cloves of garlic, finely chopped — a good pinch of ground cumin — a good pinch of dried oregano — ½ a wineglass of red wine — 2 tablespoons balsamic vinegar — 2 × 400 g tins of good-quality Italian tomatoes (I like the cherry ones best, or use passata) — a handful of fresh coriander, chopped — 2 bufala mozzarella cheeses — 4 × 175 g tuna steaks — lemon juice to serve

---

To make Place the aubergines in a colander, sprinkle them with sea salt and leave for 30 minutes. Preheat the oven to 190°C/375°F/gas 4. Wash the aubergines and pat dry, then lay them in a roasting tin. Drizzle them with olive oil and bake in the preheated oven for about 20 minutes until soft and coloured. Meanwhile gently fry the onion in a little more oil until light and golden, then add the garlic, cumin and oregano and cook for a further 2 minutes. Add a good splash of red wine and simmer until the liquid has reduced to about 2 tablespoons. Add the balsamic vinegar and let it bubble for a minute, then add the tomatoes. If they are whole, give them a squeeze between your hands to crush them. Stir in half the coriander. Simmer until the juices have evaporated and you have a rich, thick sauce.

When the aubergines are done, layer them with the tomato mixture in 4 small ovenproof dishes and put them back in the oven for 5–6 minutes. Break up the mozzarella with your hands and put some on top of each dish. Put back in the oven until the cheese has melted and is bubbling. Finish with a slick of olive oil and a final sprinkling of coriander.

While the aubergines are baking, cook the tuna. Preheat a grill plate for 10 minutes until hot. Lightly oil the tuna and cook each steak for 2–3 minutes each side, until nicely charred but still medium rare on the inside.

To serve Put each tuna steak on a serving plate, drizzle with a little olive oil, a sprinkling of sea salt and a squeeze of lemon, and place a pot of baked aubergines next to it.

Salt Cod Lasagne

This dish is based upon the recipe for creamy salt cod with onions, mozzarella and parsley. It makes a cracking family supper and is a great one for large numbers.

You will need (serves 4-6) 12–15 lasagne sheets (buy those marked 'no pre-cooking needed') — a saucepan of creamy salt cod with onions but without the mozzarella topping (see page 60) — 500 ml tomato passata — 2 bufala mozzarella cheeses — basil leaves — olive oil — freshly ground black pepper

To make Preheat the oven to 200°C/400°F/gas 6, then simply layer pasta and salt cod in an ovenproof dish until you get to the top. I like to do about 4 layers. Pour the passata over the top and bake in the preheated oven for 20 minutes. Remove the dish from the oven, break up the mozzarella and scatter evenly over the top, then put back in the oven for a further 10 minutes. Sprinkle with lots of torn basil leaves, olive oil and freshly ground black pepper and serve.

Zarzuela - a Spanish Style Fish Stew

Fish stews vary around the Mediterranean, but they are all reliant upon good fresh fish and simple local flavours. In Spain they drink sherry and naturally use it when cooking too. They have ripe tomatoes and dried peppers, which give a distinct Spanish flavour. Zarzuela means 'theatrical' and I guess the name has been used for this dish because of the medley of things going on. It's a nice dish.

At the fishmonger's 'Four langoustines, four prawns, a hake fillet about 150 grams, a piece of monkfish fillet about 150 grams, sixteen mussels, sixteen clams and a medium squid, cleaned.' If there are langoustines but no prawns use more langoustines, and vice versa. If there are no clams use cockles, and if no mussels use more clams. Get the best selection you can. I like to use small shore or velvet crabs in this dish as they are one of my favourites.

You will need (serves 4) 1 wineglass of white wine — ½ a wineglass of Manzanilla or fino sherry — 2 bay leaves, fresh if possible — 16 clams — 16 mussels — olive oil — 1 onion, finely chopped — 2 cloves of garlic, finely chopped — 300 g ripe tomatoes or a 400 g tin of good-quality Italian tomatoes, drained — 1 tablespoon tomato purée — a pinch of paprika — 1 small dried chilli — 150 g hake fillet — 150 g monkfish fillet — 1 medium squid, cleaned — 4 langoustines — 4 prawns — plain flour — ½ a wineglass of Pernod or Ricard — 500 ml water — a handful of fresh parsley — sea salt and freshly ground black pepper

---

To make Put the wine, sherry and bay leaves into a large pan. Bring to the boil, add the clams and mussels, and cook until they have opened (discard any that don't). Remove and set aside, keeping the liquid. Heat a little olive oil in another pan and gently fry the onion and garlic without browning. Add the tomatoes and continue to cook until they have melted. Add the tomato purée, paprika and chilli and cook until you have a rich, thick sauce.

Cut the fish fillets and squid into rough chunks. Heat some olive oil in a frying pan or a casserole dish large enough to hold all the ingredients. Lightly dust the fish, langoustines, prawns and squid in flour and fry until golden. Add the Pernod or Ricard, and either flame or boil it until the alcohol burns off. Add the tomato sauce, the wine and sherry that the clams were steamed in and enough of the water to just cover the fish. Stir together and simmer for 15 minutes. Stir in the parsley, season with sea salt and freshly ground black pepper, and serve.

To serve Give everybody a nice big bowl, and have a plate of slices of bread rubbed with a cut tomato and a garlic clove, drizzled with your best olive oil. Put a slice of bread in the bottom of each bowl and spoon the stew over the top.

Razor Clams with Parsley, Garlic and Hazelnuts

Razor clams seem to be getting into the popularity charts and more and more restaurants and fishmongers are selling them. I think it is because people have eaten them abroad and also, they look intriguing, making the more adventurous eater want to try them. They can look pretty strange – when they are really fresh they hang out of the ends of their shells when they are in their bundles, and it looks as if they are all waving at you! A quick prod will see them retract inside the shell. I like the smaller ones as I think they are the sweetest, however I wouldn't turn my nose up at a plate of large, simply grilled clams.

They are treated in the same way as mussels and other clams, so a bit of wine, garlic and parsley and a gentle steaming would be a good way to cook them. Their texture is quite firm but they are really juicy. I added a paste of crushed hazelnuts and parsley to a pan of bubbling clams and it really worked. If you manage to get razor clams no bigger than your middle finger, steam them with garlic, wine and parsley and toss them with spaghetti.

At the fishmonger's 'Eight medium razor clams.' They are normally sold in bunches of eight to ten. I think this serves between two and three people, but it depends on the size of the clams, and your own appetite. Make sure they are tightly closed, oozing from the end and not spread wide open like a book, with a shrivelled-up clam inside.

You will need (serves 2-3) olive oil — 2 plump cloves of garlic, finely chopped — 1 shallot, finely chopped — 100 ml white wine — 2 bay leaves — 8 razor clams — 25 g hazelnuts — a handful of fresh parsley, chopped — a pinch of salt — optional: a few fresh breadcrumbs — 1–2 lemons

To make Use a wide frying or sauté pan for this dish, preferably with a lid. If you don't have a lid, a plate or a chopping board will do to cover the pan for a few minutes while the clams are cooking. Pour a little olive oil into the pan and gently fry the garlic and shallot over a medium heat until golden. Add the wine and the bay leaves and bring to the boil for 2–3 minutes to allow the alcohol and some of the harshness of the wine to evaporate. Add the clams and cover the pan. While the clams are cooking, which will take about 4–5 minutes, smash up the hazelnuts with the parsley and a pinch of salt in a pestle and mortar, or a small hand-held food processor. When the clams have opened (discard any that don't), remove the bay leaves, put the clams on to plates and then add the parsley and hazelnut mixture to the pan and allow it to cook for a minute or two. You will be left with a thick juicy paste as the nuts start to absorb the flavour in the pan. If you think there is still too much juice add a few fresh breadcrumbs. Spoon this mixture over the clams and finish under the grill for a minute to crisp up, then add a squeeze of lemon.

To serve I like mashed potatoes with these clams, but they also just make a meal in themselves. The plate can be garnished with nothing more than a wedge of lemon and a sprig of parsley.

Try this too . . . If you like the flavour of nuts, try adding a few almonds too. Or add a roasted pepper to the pestle and mortar with the parsley and hazelnuts and stir that in. If you like razor clams but can't eat the nuts, just use breadcrumbs. Another thing that works well is a few small chunks of smoked pancetta or bacon, fried with the garlic and shallot at the beginning. You can do so much with these wonderful shellfish.but can't eat the nuts, just use breadcrumbs. Another thing that works well is a few small chunks of smoked pancetta or bacon, fried with the garlic and shallot at the beginning. You can do so much with these wonderful shellfish.

Special Occasions:
The Ocean's Élite

These recipes use ingredients such as Dover sole, bass and large turbot which will always be expensive. The quality of these fish caught in our waters is so good that they are in constant demand across the world, which therefore drives up the price. If turbot is your thing – and it is mine – wait until the end of July and into August, when there always seems to be plenty of it around and there are better landings of large fish which will give you the most delicious, thick steaks to roast with rosemary and serve with nothing more than a few runner beans and hollandaise sauce. The price drops then too.

Another fish to look out for is the first of the year's wild salmon, expensive and justifiably so. I look forward to May when I can get my hands on a mature, locally caught fish. All I do is put it into a pan of water with a bay leaf, a splash of wine, some peppercorns and some chopped carrot and celery, bring it to the boil, then turn off the heat and leave it to cool overnight. Next day, I peel off the skin to reveal the rich moist flesh and eat it with fresh mayonnaise and a handful of watercress; for me this is a special day.

Expect diver-caught scallops to be expensive; would you go underwater to gather them? The larger brill and turbot and bass get, the higher the price. This doesn't apply to Dover soles, though – they fall in price the bigger they get. I think they are a bargain and delicious to eat.

Lobsters are always expensive (avoid them at Christmas, the prices are ridiculous). If you don't mind having a lobster with a claw missing, ask your fishmonger for a cripple – it will be cheaper and will still grill and taste the same as one with two claws.

If you are choosing a recipe from this chapter go right back to the beginning of the book and look at pages 7-11, which will help you to buy and enjoy the fish you are looking for in its best condition.

Baked Sea Bass with Roasted Whole Garlic, Rosemary and Chilli

Any fish that is baked in a bag will give you great results. Everything is kicking off: you bake, steam and poach all at the same time and the juices are amazing. Add whatever flavours you like – it is a really flexible way of cooking and you can serve it straight from the bag.

At the fishmonger's 'One wild sea bass weighing about 1.25 kilos, scaled and gutted.'

You will need (serves 4) a few sprigs of fresh rosemary (thyme is good too) —
1 × 1.25 kg sea bass — 1 small dried chilli — 6 whole cloves of garlic, skin left on — sea salt
— 50 ml olive oil — ½ a wineglass of dry white wine — 1 lemon

To make Preheat the oven to 200°C/400°F/gas 6. Put a piece of turkey-size tinfoil, about 70–80 centimetres long, on to a work surface and cover with a layer of parchment paper. Fold over each edge about 2.5 centimetres, so that the foil and parchment paper are secured together at the edges. Put a couple of sprigs of rosemary in the belly cavity of the fish and a couple in the centre of the parchment. Lay the fish on the parchment and crumble the chilli over the top. Lightly crush the garlic cloves by putting the flat side of a knife on top and giving it a thump with your hand, then put them on and around the fish. Sprinkle with sea salt. Lift up the edges of the foil to keep everything in and add the olive oil and wine. Now encase the fish in the foil – it should be in a loose bag but sealed tightly, enabling it to steam. Place it on a roasting tray and bake in the preheated oven for 35 minutes.

To serve Carefully undo the bag, folding back the sides to make the fish easy to get at. Squeeze a little lemon over the top and give everyone a plate so they can help themselves. A green salad and a bowl of spuds is all you need as an accompaniment.

Try this too ... and you must ... If you enjoyed the recipe above then you must try this. Preheat the oven to 200°C/400°F/gas 6. Lay out a piece of turkey-size tinfoil about 1 metre long, cover it with parchment as above, and on it put a big pile of mussels, clams, raw prawns, langoustines, queen scallops and small crabs (in fact just about anything in a shell). Throw in some whole unpeeled garlic cloves, a few cherry tomatoes, a few sprigs of thyme. Fold up the sides and add a really good splash of dry white wine and some olive oil. Seal tightly and bake in the preheated oven for 20–25 minutes. Put it straight on the table and open up the foil. Sprinkle with chopped parsley and a squeeze of lemon juice and you will have the most magnificent pile of hot shellfish in the middle of your table for everybody to get stuck into.

Lemon or Dover Sole with Butter, Lemon and Parsley

Both Lemon and Dover sole are highly prized and delicious fish. Over the years they have been cooked in many ways, but for me the best way of all, and the simplest, is to lightly dust them with flour and gently fry them in butter, finished with lemon juice and fresh parsley.

At the fishmonger's 'A Lemon (or Dover) sole, weighing 450 grams.' If you are buying Lemon sole, there is no need to have it skinned as the skin is delicious and perfectly edible; but if you are buying Dover sole ask for it to be skinned both sides. 450 grams is the prime size for sole, as it serves one person perfectly, so allow one fish of this size each. The problem is that this is the size restaurants want and therefore the price is always higher. However, in the early part of the year when huge fish (which we call 'doormats') are caught the price is slightly cheaper.

You will need (per person) 1 × 450 g sole — plain flour for dusting — 75 g unsalted butter — sea salt — juice of 1 lemon — a small handful of fresh parsley, finely chopped

---

To make Flour both sides of the fish, then hold it by its head and give it a gentle slap either side to remove any excess. In a frying pan large enough to take the fish (if you don't have one, simply cut the fish in half, I can't think of another way), put 50 g of the butter and melt until it is gently foaming but not boiling. Add a pinch of sea salt, stir, then lay the fish in the pan on what was the dark side first – this is the fattest side and the side that you will serve uppermost. Fry gently for 7–8 minutes until the fish is crisp and golden. Turn it over and continue to fry for a further 5–6 minutes. Remove from the pan on to a plate. Add the remaining butter to the pan, turn the heat up, and allow the butter to foam until it starts to smell of hazelnuts and turns a light golden brown. Remove from the heat and add salt to taste. Add a good squeeze of lemon juice and the parsley, spoon once over the fish, and serve the rest separately. I never like to see my fish *drowned* in butter unless it's at my choice.

To serve Boiled potatoes are all you need with this.

Try this too . . . This is a simple way to cook small flat fish. Look out for small brill, dabs, which are delicious and can be a bargain (you can have a few as they are quite small), lemon sole, which don't need to be skinned, or a nice fresh Brixham plaice.

Pan-roasted Sea Bass with Sea Salt, Garlic and Rosemary

Sea bass has become very popular. Farmed bass is more consistently available, and much of it comes from France and Greece, but while the flavour of a farmed sea bass is good, it will never be the same as that of a wild fish.

Pan-roasting is an easy method of cooking. It allows you to get a nice crisp skin from the initial searing, and of course you have a wonderful ready-made sauce to spoon over the top. I enjoy cooking this dish most with a thick fillet cut from fish that 'Phil the Bass' has just delivered to us. Phil has a full-time job but is a mad keen bass fisherman – he takes his small boat off Tenby to secret locations (at least he won't tell us where he goes) and fills his Volvo with the most magnificent fish you will ever see, all rod-and-line caught. They come in all sizes but the larger fish taste superior.

At the fishmonger's 'Two fillets of wild sea bass, about 175 grams each.' A whole fish weighing about 450–500 grams will give you two fillets which will be big enough.

You will need (serves 2) a glug of olive oil — 2 × 175 g fillets of sea bass — a splash of white wine — 25 g butter — 2 sprigs of fresh rosemary — 2 plump cloves of garlic, in their skins, bashed with a knife — lemon juice — sea salt

---

To make Heat the oil in a heavy-based frying pan with a tight-fitting lid and lay the sea bass fillets in the pan, skin-side down. Fry for 3–4 minutes until the skin is crisp and golden. Turn the fish over, add a splash of wine and allow the alcohol to evaporate and sizzle – you should only have a few tablespoons of juice left in the pan. Turn the heat down and add the butter, rosemary and garlic, then cover and simmer gently for a further 7–8 minutes. Remove the fish from the pan and place on serving plates. Add a squeeze of lemon to the pan juices, season to taste, then spoon over the fish. The garlic should be moist and creamy when mashed with a fork and should be served with the fish.

To serve French beans tossed with a few chopped raw shallots are good, as are mashed or boiled potatoes.

Try this too ... Fillets of sea bream, gurnard and haddock are exceptionally good cooked this way. Any of these fish are also great cooked simply with garlic, chilli and thyme.

Lobster Caesar

This is a good way to stretch a lobster! A lobster weighing about 750 g will comfortably feed 4 in this recipe and make a delicious light lunch. You can keep it just to lobster, or add some chunks of crab meat and the occasional anchovy.

At the fishmonger's 'One native lobster, weighing about 750 grams.' Buying it live and cooking it yourself is best, but if you haven't got the time or don't feel like doing it, get your fishmonger to show you it live and pop back later when he has cooked it. Eat it as soon as you can to enjoy it at its best.

You will need 1 × 750 g lobster — 1 large cos lettuce — 3 anchovy fillets in oil — 1 clove of garlic — 1 tablespoon mustard — 1 egg yolk — 1 tablespoon Worcestershire Sauce — 50 g parmesan cheese, shaved into thin strips with a potato peeler — 100 ml vegetable oil — 100 ml olive oil — a few tablespoons cold water — freshly made croûtons (thin slices of ciabatta brushed with olive oil and placed in a hot oven until crisp, then rubbed with a garlic clove on both sides before being cut into bite-sized chunks)

To make First prepare the lobster. Snap off the claws from the body and twist the tail away from the head. Scoop any dark brown meat and red coral from inside the head and set aside to add to the dressing. Turn the lobster tail upside down with the legs facing you and with a pair of scissors snip down either side so the tail meat can be removed whole. Then slice it into thin discs. Give the claws a good crack with the heel of a knife and remove the meat.

Prepare the lettuce by cutting off the thick root, keeping the leaves whole and washing them thoroughly in cold water. Leave to drain and then place them in a large bowl.

Into your food processor put the anchovy fillets, the brown lobster meat and coral from the head, the garlic, mustard, egg yolk, Worcestershire Sauce and 3–4 shavings of parmesan. Blitz this mixture to a smooth paste. Mix together the vegetable oil and olive oil – the vegetable oil will stop the olive oil being too fruity and dominant in the dressing. With the motor running, gradually add the mixed oils until you have a thick emulsion. Then add cold water to lighten it.

Toss the lettuce leaves in the dressing, add the croûtons, sprinkle the lobster chunks and parmesan shavings on top and serve.

Lobster with Manzanilla and Tarragon

Manzanilla is a beautiful sherry from a magical place called Sanlucar de Barrameda on the Spanish coast. It has a salty tang which is said to come from the sea air. It is one of my favourite drinks and it works well with gently sautéd lobster.

At the fishmonger's 'One 750 gram live lobster.' It is best to use a raw lobster, but you can use a cooked one if you shorten the cooking time to about 7–8 minutes in total. If you can't get lobster, use a small cooked crab weighing about 500 grams.

You will need (serves 2) 1 × 750 g lobster — 30 g unsalted butter — sea salt and freshly ground black pepper — 2 cloves of garlic, finely chopped — 1 small glass of Manzanilla — 1 tomato, deseeded and chopped — a handful of fresh tarragon, chopped — 6 tablespoons double cream

---

To make To kill and cut up your lobster, see page 54.

In a heavy-based sauté or frying pan, gently melt the butter and stir in a pinch of sea salt and the garlic. Add the chunks of lobster including the claws but reserving the meat from the head, and turn them over and over in the butter until well coated. Do not allow the butter to become too hot or the garlic will burn. Cook gently for 10–12 minutes.

Add the Manzanilla to the pan; it can be overpowering, so don't use it all at once – add a bit, stir it in, then taste. Cook until all the alcohol has evaporated, about 2–3 minutes. Add the reserved lobster meat from the head, the chopped tomato and the tarragon, stirring well, and last of all stir in a few tablespoons of double cream. Season with freshly ground black pepper and serve.

To serve Use a big bowl that will really show off the lobster. Pile it up in the middle and spoon the pan juices over the top. It is quite rich so all you need is a fresh green or tomato and onion salad and a glass of Manzanilla. Good crusty bread is great for mopping up the juices from the bowl.

Try this too ... This works with fresh langoustines and prawns. Mussels would also work well cooked this way, but cover the pan at the start of cooking, still on a gentle heat, to allow them to steam open in their own juices (discard any that don't open).

Raw Oysters with Horseradish Cream and Caviar

There are many ways to serve oysters and the more complicated they get the less delicious they become. While there are some hot dishes that I really enjoy serving, my favourites are those that rely on raw fresh oysters. Caviar is a wonderful indulgence, and a teaspoon of it sitting on an oyster is amazing. This recipe, with fresh, grated horseradish, is delicious, and half a dozen of these should be washed down with half a dozen shots of ice-cold vodka.

At the fishmonger's 'Six rock oysters.' Rock oysters are available all year round, native or wild oysters between September and April. Look out for French oysters called *fine de claire*, which are really pure and special.

You will need (serves 1) a squeeze of lemon juice — 6 tablespoons stiffly whipped cream — 1 tablespoon very finely chopped onion — 1 tablespoon freshly grated horseradish — 6 oysters — the yolk of 1 boiled egg, finely grated — 25 g sevruga or avruga caviar (make these with beluga and oscietra at your bank manager's peril)

To make Squeeze a little lemon juice into the cream to sour it, then mix in the onion and horseradish. Spoon some of this on top of each oyster in its shell, sprinkle with the grated egg yolk, then divide the caviar equally between the oysters.

To serve A bed of rock salt stops the oysters rolling over, or serve them on crushed ice.

Try this too ... If you are in a caviar mood, boil yourself a duck egg for breakfast and put a spoonful on top before dunking your soldiers. Another fun thing to do for oyster lovers: next time you pour yourself a good Martini, slip in an oyster and its juice – the alcohol cooks it, the juice freshens the Martini. You drink the drink and chew the oyster. It is also good to throw one into a spicy Bloody Mary. See what you think.

John Dory with Cured Ham, Mozzarella, Chilli and Basil Leaf

I am not usually a fan of cheese with fish, but mozzarella has its place just about anywhere. These little pieces of fish wrapped up in mozzarella, chilli and Parma ham are simple and taste great.

At the fishmonger's 'A 500 gram John Dory, filleted and skinned.' You will get 2 fillets, each of which will naturally divide into 3. It is the only fish that is like this. Pull the fillets apart where you see these natural channels in the fillet, to make 6. Plaice and lemon sole are great cooked like this too.

You will need (serves 2–3) 2 × 250 g John Dory fillets — 6 slices of Parma ham — 75 g bufala mozzarella cheese — ½ a mild fresh chilli, seeds removed and cut into thin strips (if you like a bit more heat, leave the seeds in) — good olive oil — a pinch of sea salt — juice and zest of ½ a lime — 1 clove of garlic, crushed — 6 basil leaves, shredded — 1 tomato, seeds removed and flesh roughly chopped

To make Divide each John Dory fillet into 3 pieces. Lay a slice of Parma ham flat on a chopping board and place a piece of John Dory at one end. Cut the mozzarella into 6 thin slices and place one on top of the fish. Add a few bits of chilli and roll the fish up in the ham, making sure the cheese and the chillies are held in, keeping it as tight as you can. Make 6 rolls altogether. The rolls can be refrigerated for a few hours if you wish, before cooking.

Preheat your oven to its maximum temperature.

Heat a glug of olive oil in a good heavy-based ovenproof frying pan. Add the fish rolls and fry gently for 4 minutes, until the ham is just starting to crisp underneath. Turn the fish over gently, then put the whole pan into the preheated oven and cook for 3–4 minutes. The cheese should just start to melt, the fish will be creamy and moist.

Remove the pan from the oven and divide the fish between your serving plates. Add another glug of olive oil to the pan, along with a pinch of sea salt, the lime juice and zest and the garlic, and give it all a good stir. Warm through, then stir in the basil and tomato and spoon a little over the fish.

To serve Good as a starter for 6, or a main course for 2–3. It also works well served in one dish, family-style, for everyone to help themselves. A nice peppery rocket salad is a good accompaniment.

Try this too ... Instead of the chilli, put a couple of sage leaves inside the ham. Add a bit of butter and a few more sage leaves to the pan with the oil, and finish with a squeeze of lime. Don't overdo the sage as it can be quite overpowering.

Sea Scallops Steamed over Seaweed with Herb Beurre Blanc

There is nothing like a fat, juicy scallop seared quickly in a frying pan. They are pretty versatile too: you can wrap a bit of bacon around them with a sage leaf and grill them or, as in this dish, you can leave them in their shells and simply steam them on a bed of seaweed – their flavour is fantastic.

At the fishmonger's 'A dozen diver-caught scallops in the shell.' Ask your fishmonger to clean them and leave the scallop still in the cut shell. If your fishmonger has got some oysters in, the chances are they will have been packed in seaweed and you can ask him for a handful.

You will need (serves 4) a handful of seaweed — 12 scallops in the shell — 3 shallots, very finely chopped — 50 ml white wine — 50 ml white wine vinegar — 50 ml double cream — 50 g butter — 1 tablespoon chopped fresh tarragon — 1 tablespoon chopped fresh parsley

---

To make Place the seaweed in a large pan, or a couple of roasting dishes large enough to hold the scallops in their shells, and add 565 ml of water. Bring this to the boil. The seaweed will turn green and you will get the most magnificent smell coming from the pan. Place the scallops on top of the seaweed and cover the pan. They will take about 5 minutes to steam and they will turn from opaque to a firm, milky white. Put the shallots, wine and vinegar in another saucepan and boil to reduce until only a teaspoonful of the liquid is left. Add the cream and reduce again by half. Remove from the heat and gradually whisk in the butter. Lastly add the tarragon and parsley.

To serve Remove the scallops from the pan. Lay some seaweed on each plate, place 3 scallops per person on top, and spoon just a tablespoon of the sauce over each one. If you do not have scallop shells, place 3 scallops around the edge with just a little bit of salad in the middle and spoon the sauce on or around the scallops.

Try this too ... Beurre blanc is an easy, quick and versatile sauce which works with any fish. You can vary the herbs – dill and a few capers work well. If you ever come across sea urchin roes, stir them into a basic beurre blanc.

Eating Outdoors: What's Easy and What Works

My best meals are those I've eaten outside. When I was behind the fish counter, people would talk about sardines grilled on a wood fire in the Algarve, or lobsters bought from a local fisherman and grilled on a beach in the Greek islands, or a simple selection of wild mussels in Ireland eaten just there and then on the sand. They had all been outside too.

By the sea is best, but if you live in a city the garden is the next best place to enjoy a good meal. Warm temperatures and the smell of hot coals are evocative in themselves, but marinated meats, sausages, a few parcels of roasted vegetables are about as adventurous as many people ever get. Occasionally the odd tuna steak or prawn kebab sneaks in, but I think people shy away from cooking fish in the garden because they don't know enough about it. But the sight of a fresh mackerel or sardine blistering and blackening over a fire will excite anyone, and the flavour of fish cooked over hot smouldering wood can't be beaten.

I just like to eat outdoors. I like to make a fresh prawn salad – loads of crispy iceberg lettuce, covered with handfuls of fresh prawns and a seafood sauce made from mayonnaise, tomato ketchup, Tabasco, Worcestershire Sauce and a touch of brandy or whisky. Smother it over the top of the prawns and add a good pinch of cayenne pepper and a squeeze of lemon juice. Bowls of pasta are easy too.

If there is a spell of good weather try a chilled marinated fish dish like marinated grilled herrings with roast tomato, marjoram and hot chilli. Or in the morning fry a few sardines until golden, then boil $\frac{1}{2}$ a wineglass of white wine with

½ a wineglass of white wine vinegar, a finely chopped carrot, a finely chopped stick of celery, a teaspoon of sugar, a small sliced onion and a sliced clove of garlic. Pour this over the fish while it's warm, chill until evening, tear a few basil and mint leaves over the top, pour over some olive oil and serve it with crusty bread.

With fish like sea bass, keep them whole, make a few slashes in the flesh, stuff them with rosemary and start them on a *hot* barbecue. A cool barbecue will make the fish stick. Char the skin so the herbs burn for 3–4 minutes each side, then place the whole fish, drizzled with a bit of olive oil, into a preheated hot oven and finish the cooking for 10 minutes there. With sardines, small anchovies, mackerel and squid the cooking can all be done over the coals because they are smaller and will cook more quickly. Brush squid with sweet chilli sauce or the chilli jam on page 26. Grill tuna or swordfish and serve it with the pesto on page 22. Keep it simple, keep it hot and get the oven to help with cooking big fish.

Try lobster a la plancha on the barbecue (see page 163). For another really great dish, take a small cooked lobster, cut it in half, crack the claws and remove the meat from the tail. Put a bit of garlic butter in the shell with a few tarragon leaves and put the meat back into the shell on top of this. Put the lobster, shell-side down, on the barbecue and put a casserole dish upside down over the top of it. Stuff the coals with branches of rosemary, thyme or fennel and allow the smoke to go up inside the casserole dish and permeate the lobster while the heat from the barbecue melts the butter, making the lobster rich, garlicky, moist and absolutely luxurious. It really works.

Burano Style Shrimp Cocktail

This is an amazingly simple mixture of seafood and olive oil. Use the best oil and the freshest shrimps you can get – the two are fantastic together.

At the fishmonger's '200 grams of peeled brown shrimps.' If you can only get unpeeled shrimps, allow 500 grams. Prawns are too soft and don't work well, so wait until you come across brown shrimps.

You will need (serves 4 as an appetizer) 200 g peeled brown shrimps — 1 tablespoon finely chopped parsley — a pinch of Maldon sea salt — the best olive oil you can find (I used fantastic extra virgin olive oil from Villa Rizzaldi in Verona, it's delicious – the flavour of the oil is part of the dish, so I emphasize using a really good one that you like) — lemon juice

To make Put the shrimps, parsley, sea salt and about 2 tablespoons of olive oil into a bowl and mix together. Add a few drops of lemon juice, but don't overdo it.

To serve Serve in small ramekins or as part of an appetizer plate, maybe with freshly boiled langoustines, mayonnaise and some good bread.

Fresh Bream Ceviche with Chilli, Coconut and Ginger

Ceviche is a South American preparation where fish is 'cooked' in lime juice and mixed with chopped red onion, chilli and coriander. It's particularly delicious done with raw scallops, with just a handful of mint thrown in too. This recipe uses thin slices of fresh bream, which is ace for preparing in this way. Fresh coconut, ginger and chilli make it really refreshing and it is a perfect starter in summer.

At the fishmonger's 'One 450 gram sea bream, filleted and pinboned.' Small farmed sea bass, lemon sole, turbot, brill and even mackerel work well too.

You will need (serves 2) 1 × 450 g sea bream, filleted and pinboned — juice of 2 limes — 1 tablespoon white wine vinegar or rice vinegar — 1 teaspoon sugar — salt — 1 coconut, with milk — 1 fresh red chilli, finely sliced — 1 tablespoon coriander, leaves torn — 1 tablespoon finely grated fresh root ginger

---

To make You will need a sharp knife to cut the fish into thin slices. Lay the fillets skin side down on a chopping board and take the first slice about 5 cm away from the tail, slicing diagonally. Continue to take thin slices of fish from the skin until it is all sliced.

Mix half the lime juice with the vinegar and sugar and stir until the sugar is dissolved. Put the fish into a non-metallic bowl, pour the mixture over, add a sprinkling of salt, and put in the fridge for an hour.

Drain the coconut of its milk and grate the flesh until you have about 2 heaped tablespoons. Remove the fish from the vinegar and lime juice and lay the slices on a cold serving dish. Discard the vinegar and lime juice mixture. Mix together the grated coconut, the sliced chilli, the remaining lime juice, 2–3 tablespoons of the coconut milk, the coriander and the ginger. Place a teaspoon or so of this mixture on each piece of fish, and serve.

Gazpacho with Seafood

On a hot day a cool crisp gazpacho can be just the ticket. A handful of fresh shellfish and herbs thrown in is definitely worth a try.

At the fishmonger's 'Four oysters, six mussels, a handful of clams, four langoustines and 100 grams of white crab meat.' Use any combination of shellfish you like, but try to include the oyster and the crab.

You will need (serves 4–6) 4 oysters — 6 mussels — a handful of clams — 4 langoustines — 100 g white crab meat — 1 fat clove of garlic, crushed — 1 cucumber, peeled and finely chopped — a small bunch of spring onions, thinly sliced — ½ a red onion, finely chopped — 4 really ripe tomatoes, roughly chopped — 1 red pepper, finely diced — 1 green pepper, finely diced — a small handful of tarragon, chopped — a splash of red wine vinegar — a few drops of Tabasco — 350 ml good-quality tomato juice (or make your own by blitzing fresh tomatoes and straining the juice) — a few glugs of best olive oil — sea salt and freshly ground black pepper

To make First open the oysters, mussels and clams. If you prefer not to eat them raw, lightly steam them, but make sure you add the juices to the soup. Some recipes call for the gazpacho to be smooth – if you like it this way, make it in a food processor. However, I like it chunky and crunchy. Combine the remaining ingredients, with the exception of the langoustines and crab meat, adjusting the vinegar, Tabasco, salt and pepper to your taste. Put in the fridge and chill for a few hours before serving to allow the flavours to develop. Just before serving add the oysters, mussels and clams, the langoustines (lightly boiled if you prefer them cooked), and sprinkle the white crabmeat over the top.

To serve Serve this in wide shallow bowls with a sprinkling of crunchy sea salt and a slick of your best fruity olive oil on top. Make sure you have plenty of good crusty bread.

Try this too … Experiment with other herbs like fresh basil, mint and parsley. Try adding lemon juice at the end for a really zesty flavour, or include fennel in the gazpacho. Different coloured tomatoes, both green and yellow, make a lovely addition too.

Grilled Cured Anchovies with Wild Oregano

Until about six or seven years ago you could only buy salted anchovies, which were sold in oval tins and hidden away on supermarket shelves among the red salmon and weird things like tinned crab, but now anchovies are everywhere, sold in jars or whole, still buried in salt or still fresh. The Spanish take fresh anchovies and lightly cure them in vinegar with sliced or chopped garlic. They call them *boquerones*, and I have to say that when you've eaten them in Spain with a glass of albariño or cold sherry, or even cured your own, you will see how superior they are to the factory-produced varieties (however, these can be improved by tossing them in a bit of garlic, fresh mint or chilli).

At the fishmonger's 'A kilo of fresh anchovies, filleted.' If the fishmonger is busy, it's easy to fillet them yourself. Put the fish on its belly and, starting just at the back of the head, press the back down toward the board with your thumb, gradually working toward the tail. The fish will split open and the fillets can then be peeled off and washed. You can also make this dish with small sardine or herring fillets and, if you are lucky enough, fresh whitebait.

You will need (serves 6) 2 plump cloves of garlic, thinly sliced — salt — 1 kg fresh anchovies, filleted — 1 tablespoon wild oregano (on the branch if possible) — 250 ml white wine vinegar — 100 ml very good olive oil — optional: fresh chopped parsley — 1 small shallot, finely chopped

To make Make sure the grill is hot. If you are using a grill plate make sure you preheat it for at least 10 minutes before you cook, otherwise the fish will stick. Lay the garlic in the bottom of a non-metallic dish and sprinkle with a pinch of salt. Grill the anchovies skin side down for about a minute until nicely charred. Lay them next to each other, flesh-side down, on top of the garlic. When they are all grilled, sprinkle with half the oregano and then pour on the vinegar, making sure that all the anchovies are in contact with it. Refrigerate for 4–5 minutes, then drain off as much of the vinegar as you can by tilting the dish. Sprinkle the fish with the remaining oregano, pour over the olive oil, add a sprinkling of chopped fresh parsley and the shallot if you wish and serve.

To serve I like to serve these on round plates, with 8 or 9 fillets per person arranged like spokes around the plate. Make sure everybody gets plenty of the garlic and oil, and have a bottle of really good olive oil to hand. You will need good chunks of bread to mop up the oil and lightly pickled garlic.

Try this too . . . If you like more of a sweet and sour flavour, dissolve a few tablespoons of caster sugar in the vinegar before pouring it on to the anchovies, adding a few shredded sun-dried tomatoes, pine nuts and raisins or a pinch of good-quality saffron.

Baked Sardine Fillets with Basil Leaf, Pine Nuts and Dried Tomatoes

This is a nice quick way with sardines and is made with ingredients you'll have in the store-cupboard.

At the fishmonger's 'Eight large sardines, scaled and filleted.' If you can't find good sardines, use mackerel or herring fillets. Tuna steaks work well this way too.

You will need (serves 4) 1 onion, finely sliced — 1 clove of garlic, finely chopped — olive oil — 4 tablespoons red wine vinegar — ½ teaspoon sugar — a splash of white wine — 1 tablespoon pine nuts, lightly toasted — 1 tablespoon raisins — 3–4 pieces of sun-dried tomato, lightly shredded (I like the ones in oil best) — 1 small dried chilli — 1 tablespoon fresh white breadcrumbs — sea salt — a handful of shredded fresh basil leaves — 8 sardines, scaled and filleted — 1 lemon

---

To make First make the topping. Fry the onion and garlic in olive oil until softened and golden. Add the red wine vinegar and the sugar, stir well and reduce until evaporated, then add the white wine and cook until it has reduced to almost nothing. Add the pine nuts, raisins and sun-dried tomatoes and crumble in the chilli. Then stir in the breadcrumbs and fry for 3–4 minutes until they have absorbed the flavours and juices in the pan, become slightly crisp and you are left with a loose stuffing. Lastly season with sea salt and add the basil leaves. This can be made a few hours in advance if you wish.

Preheat the oven to 200°C/400°F/gas 6. Heat a grill plate for 10 minutes. Lightly oil the fish on the skin side, sprinkle with sea salt, and grill for 2–3 minutes on the skin side only until charred. Place the fillets side by side, skin side down, on a baking tray lightly coated with olive oil. Spoon the stuffing mixture over the fillets and bake in the preheated oven for 5–6 minutes. Finish with a squeeze of lemon juice.

To serve Serve 2 sardines per person, straight from the dish, with a fresh green salad dressed with nothing more than olive oil and lemon juice.

Try this too ... Put some of the stuffing on each fillet, curl them up, secure with a cocktail stick, and bake the same way. These are delicious served cold as well. Dress with vinegar and oil before serving.

Herrings in Spiced Cream Sauce

Herrings are about the most underrated fish you can buy. Their flesh is moist and creamy. They are the best fish for pickling and curing.

At the fishmonger's 'Six herrings, filleted.' You can make this dish with mackerel and small sardines, but herrings are worth waiting for as I think they work best.

You will need (serves 2–3) 6 herrings, filleted — 200 g rock salt — 2 large onions, thinly sliced — 4 dried bay leaves — 1 teaspoon black peppercorns, crushed in a pestle and mortar — 8 allspice berries, crushed — 1 tablespoon caster sugar — 250 ml white wine vinegar — 300 ml double cream — a handful of chopped fresh dill

To make Cover the herrings with the salt and leave in the fridge overnight. Scrape off the salt and soak the herrings in cold water for 8 hours, changing the water at least once during soaking. Taste a little of the herring to see how salty it is; if it is too salty simply soak it for longer.

Blanch the onions in boiling water for 2–3 minutes, then drain. Toss with the bay leaves and spices. Cut the herrings into bite-sized chunks and put them into a sterilized jar in alternate layers with the onions. Onions should be your last layer. Dissolve the sugar in the vinegar then add the cream and dill. Pour this mixture into the jar to completely cover the herrings. Put into the fridge for 3 days, after which time they will be ready to eat.

To serve Sliced rye or wholemeal bread, chopped hard-boiled eggs and onions are all you need.

Try this too ... Add some mustard powder or curry paste to the cream before mixing with the vinegar, and stir in a handful of chopped fresh coriander before pouring over the herrings.

Marinated Grilled Herrings with Roast Tomato, Marjoram and Hot Chilli

Oily fish like herring and mackerel really stand up to spicy, hot flavours, and they also pickle extremely well. Most countries have their own version of escabeche, fish which has been first cooked and then marinated in vinegar with vegetables and aromatics. It is usually dredged in flour and fried and is particularly delicious. I took a few fat herrings and grilled them over a barbecue (you can use a grill plate) until the skins were nicely blackened and the insides creamy and moist, then marinated them in fiery chilli and marjoram. Try to buy wild marjoram (otherwise known as oregano), as it is much more fragrant. The chillies in the cure are the small dried ones you daren't put in your mouth whole. They add heat to the dish.

At the fishmonger's 'Four fresh herrings, scaled, gutted and heads removed.' If there are any roes, keep them and see page 63. Sardines and mackerel fillets are good prepared this way too, as are fresh anchovies. Thinking about it, tuna or swordfish would be good as well.

You will need (serves 2) 4 herrings, scaled, gutted and heads removed — 75 ml good olive oil — a few pinches of sea salt — freshly ground black pepper — 2 cloves of garlic, finely sliced — 4 small dried chillies, crushed in a pestle and mortar, or a teaspoon of chilli flakes (but watch out!) — 1 teaspoon dried marjoram or oregano — 200 ml red wine vinegar — a few tablespoons sherry vinegar — optional: 2 roasted tomato halves (see page 44) or chopped fresh tomato — a handful of fresh marjoram or oregano leaves

---

To make Brush the herrings lightly with a little of the oil and season with salt and freshly ground black pepper. Put them on the grill or barbecue for 3 minutes either side, or until the skin is nicely charred and blackened. Set aside.

Put the sliced garlic into a non-metallic dish with a pinch of salt and half the chilli and dried marjoram or oregano. Place the fish on top then sprinkle over the vinegars. Scatter the remaining dried chilli and marjoram or oregano over the top. Put in the fridge for an hour, turning the fish once half-way through.

Drain off as much of the vinegar as you can. Squeeze the tomatoes in your hand (I love this bit), over the fish, so they are covered in their juice. Pour over the olive oil. Chill for a further hour to allow the flavours to develop, then remove from the fridge and allow to come to room temperature before sprinkling with fresh marjoram or oregano and freshly ground black pepper.

To serve Just put the whole dish on the table for people to help themselves, making sure there is plenty of bread to mop up the juices. A nice cooling chopped cucumber and mint salad is delicious with this.

Try this too ... Play around with the herbs – try lots more garlic, plenty of fresh parsley or lemon zest. Or fry the fish until nice and golden instead of grilling.

Lobster a la Plancha:
the Perfect Grilled Lobster

Lobster a la plancha is nothing more exotic than lobster on a grill. The *plancha* is a flat grill plate used in Spain and the Balearics to cook meat, fish and vegetables.

I recently breakfasted on lobster a la plancha after a night at the wholesale fish market, the Mercabarna in Barcelona, one of the biggest and best markets I have ever seen. Afterwards I went to the fabulous Boqueria market on the Ramblas, which is where everyone buys their food. Standing at a bar in the market at seven in the morning with my mate Roy, after a few shots of local spirit and some Spanish brandy, I watched fresh lobster from the market cooking on the *plancha* while the man behind the bar, who I thought should have been watching the lobster, continued to pour drinks, comfortable with the cooking going on behind him. His relaxed style said a lot about the Mediterranean way of life, the way it should be.

The lobster was only turned at the last minute, so the shell kept it fantastically firm, moist and sweet. It was brushed with a little olive oil, sea salt, garlic and parsley and we were given a little pot of rich all-i-oli for dunking chunks of lobster into.

At the fishmonger's 'A live native lobster, about 750 grams.' Mediterranean lobsters are a different species from our native ones – in England we call them crawfish, the French call them langoustes or spiny lobsters. The main difference is that they have no claws, are brown in colour and have a bigger, more powerful tail. The meat is fantastic, but I still hold our native British lobster in the highest regard.

You will need (serves 2) 1 × 750 g live lobster — sea salt — a few glugs of good extra virgin olive oil — 2 cloves of fresh garlic, crushed — a handful of fresh parsley, chopped — zest and juice of ½ a lemon — all-i-oli (see page 25)

To make To kill and cut up your lobster, see page 54. Preheat the oven to 200°C/400°F/gas 6. Give the claws a crack with the back of a heavy knife, and put them into the preheated oven when you start to grill the rest of the lobster. They will be ready when the rest of the lobster is done.

Get your grill plate really hot and put the lobster halves shell side down on to it. As the lobster cooks, the shell will start to change colour from a dark blue to a vibrant orange and you'll see the juices in the shell just shimmering as they warm through. Instead of the lobster being fiercely grilled and becoming dry, it is being poached in its own juices and the sea water in the shell. Grill it on this side for around 8–10 minutes, then sprinkle a little sea salt over the flesh, carefully turn it over, and grill it for a further 4–5 minutes.

Mix together the olive oil, garlic, parsley, lemon zest and juice. You should have a thick oily green paste flecked with yellow. Put the lobster on a serving plate and spoon over the oil mixture to your taste.

To serve When I serve this I put just a little of the oil mixture on top of the lobster and leave the rest in a bowl for dunking. If you want to make all-i-oli, see page 25. Serve half a lobster as a starter or light lunch and a whole one as a main course.

Roasted Langoustines with Ginger, Chilli and Coriander Butter

Roasted whole or just split and grilled over a wood fire, langoustines are my absolute favourites. Live ones are best, as their flesh is firmer and sweeter. Ginger works particularly well in this butter, which is smothered all over the shellfish and just makes you want to lick, suck and chew every last bit of sweet meat there is to be had.

At the fishmonger's 'A dozen large, live langoustines.' If you can't get langoustines, buy yourself a live lobster (see page 54). Freshly boiled crab, warmed through in the oven and tossed in lots of this butter, would be good too.

You will need (serves 2) 12 langoustines — 50 g fresh root ginger, peeled and finely chopped — 2 mild red chillies, deseeded and finely chopped — a handful of fresh coriander — juice and zest of 1 lime — 100 ml ginger beer — 250 g unsalted butter, softened — sea salt

---

To make If your langoustines are still alive, see page 72. Put the langoustines on their backs, then take a sharp knife and cut them from the head to the tail but without going right through the top shell. The langoustines can then be opened out flat, with your thumbs. They look nice on the plate like this, and it makes them more accessible.

Put the ginger, chillies, coriander, lime juice and zest and ginger beer into a food processor and blend to a smooth, fine paste. Stir this mixture into the softened butter and season with plenty of sea salt.

Put the langoustines shell side down on a grill plate or barbecue, or in a hot, heavy-based frying pan. Cook for 4–5 minutes – the shells will start to char (and smell good) but the meat will be protected. Lastly turn them over for a minute to just sear the flesh side. Put all the langoustines and any juices from the pan into a big mixing bowl. Melt the flavoured butter, season with more salt or lime juice if needed, and pour over the langoustines. Toss as if you were dressing a salad, then pile the langoustines on a big plate and dig in.

To serve This is lovely to eat outdoors with grilled courgette salad with mint leaf and garlic (see page 189).

Try this too ... Good garlic butter (see page 28) is great with these langoustines and you can spice it up a bit by adding a little fennel, lots of lemon juice and fresh mint.

Salt Cod with Sweet Peppers, Black Olives, Mint and Parsley Leaf

I think most people are a bit daunted by salt cod. A few years ago it became fashionable in restaurants every-where, and every dish I tried made me realize why people shied away from it. In pursuit of the salt cod experi-ence I travelled to Portugal and Catalonia, where it is almost a national dish. I couldn't believe my eyes when I walked into a Portuguese supermarket and there was a counter at least ten metres long piled high with nothing but salt cod in all kinds of shapes and sizes.

Sometimes I marinate salt cod in olive oil and garlic before I cook it. It really does impart a great flavour to the fish. This is one of my favourite salt cod recipes, although I have eaten some wonderful combinations with honey, battered and deep-fried, and in salads with artichokes and fresh peas. To salt and prepare your own cod, see page 36.

At the fishmonger's '400 grams of thick salt cod.' The thicker the cod the more luxurious the texture will be, as you will get lovely big white creamy flakes. Sometimes the commercially produced cod available here can be too hard, and I prefer to salt my own.

You will need (serves 4) good olive oil — 1 onion, thinly sliced — 1 red pepper, thinly sliced — 2 cloves of garlic, crushed — a splash of red wine vinegar — 400 g salt cod, soaked and ready to cook — 7–8 black olives — a small handful of fresh mint, chopped — a small handful of fresh parsley, chopped — juice of ½ a lemon — freshly ground black pepper

---

To make Pour 3–4 glugs of good olive oil into a wide, heavy-based pan until the bottom of the pan is com-pletely covered. Add the onion and the pepper and sweat slowly over a very gentle heat for about 15–20 minutes until softened but not brown. Add the garlic and cook for another 3–4 minutes. Add the vinegar and allow to reduce.

Take the salt cod out of its soaking water, remove the skin and cut it into chunks. Add the fish to the pan with another glug of oil and stir gently. Add the olives and continue to cook for 3–4 minutes. The cod will break up but don't worry, it is meant to be like this. Add the mint and parsley and stir in well.

This dish is particularly good eaten cold, especially on a hot day, in the garden. What I do is add a bit more olive oil and keep it in the fridge overnight.

To serve Put a small pile of cod in the middle of each plate, with maybe a few rocket leaves. Squeeze a little lemon juice over the top and sprinkle with freshly ground black pepper. The olive oil that the dish has been cooked in is great for dunking crusty bread or lumps of raw vegetables, such as fennel, onions or pepper. A bowl of aïoli is also good on the side.

Try this too ... Use different coloured peppers. Or add some fresh chilli or a few salted capers, or a pinch of paprika as Catalans do. You can toss this with pasta, spread it on toast and just warm it under the grill with some good oil, or add a few tablespoons to an omelette.

Seafood Salad with Fresh Herbs and Olive Oil

Unfortunately the words 'seafood salad' always bring to mind the vinegary seafood mixtures so often on offer these days. While these can be tasty, they are really not the full ticket. There is nothing like freshly cooked seafood tossed in fruity olive oil, garlic, lemon juice, and the juices and sea water from freshly cooked shellfish.

At the fishmonger's One fresh medium squid, weighing 175 grams, cleaned, 8 tightly closed mussels, 8 tightly closed surf clams, and 100 grams of monkfish fillet.' Mussels or clams are essential, because their juices add so much to the flavour of the dressing. Avoid using softer fish like cod or haddock, as it will break up during cooking.

You will need (serves 2) a dash of white wine — 1 clove of garlic, finely sliced — a glug of good olive oil — 8 mussels, tightly closed — 8 surf clams, tightly closed — 1 heaped tablespoon chopped fresh fennel — 1 medium squid, cleaned and cut into fine rings — 100 g monkfish fillet, cut into small chunks — 6 medium prawns — 6 cherry tomatoes, cut into quarters — a small handful of fresh basil leaves, chopped — a squeeze of lemon juice — sea salt — lettuce leaves, for serving

To make Add a dash of white wine to an empty pan and then add the garlic. Boil for a minute, then add a really good glug of olive oil. Put the mussels and clams into the pot, cover, and cook until they have all opened. Remove the shellfish from the liquid, discarding any that have remained closed, and put them into a bowl to cool. Add the fennel, squid, monkfish and prawns to the liquid with another good glug of olive oil. Simmer gently, and I mean gently, for 3–4 minutes until the fish just turns from opaque to white and firms up. When cooking fish, think of the fish as being jelly-like and the cooking process just setting it.

Remove the squid and monkfish from the liquid and put them into the bowl with the mussels and clams. Remove the meat from the clams and the mussels, discarding the shells. When the liquid is cooled add the tomatoes, basil and lemon juice and toss together with the shellfish. Season with sea salt to taste. Either chill until really cold, or serve at room temperature.

To serve Because this is fresh and summery I like to serve it on a big white plate on top of whole lettuce leaves, like cos or a simple round lettuce. It doesn't really need anything else except a sunny day and a bottle of chilled wine.

Try this too . . . A nice little twist to this is to replace the fennel with lemon grass, add lots of chopped chilli, replace the basil with coriander or Thai basil, and the lemon juice with lime. Or you can add a few more vegetables such as chopped cucumber and peppers and add a dash of red wine vinegar to the liquid so that you almost have a gazpacho-style seafood salad combination.

Building and Serving
a Fruits de Mer

The French are masters of the *fruits de mer*, as anybody who has visited Paris, or been to the French ports, will know. If you order it in England, what you get is called a 'platter'. I really hate that word. It conjures up a few frozen pink prawns, a bit of crab, some mussels, cooked and chilled hours earlier, and, in the worst cases, cooked squid, marinated herrings and other things which just shouldn't be there.

A *fruits de mer* is an occasion in itself: it is grand, it shouts out loud for you to enjoy yourself. It can be long and lingering and, if it is put together properly, it is without doubt one of the finest eating experiences you can have. What we are talking about here is a pile of the freshest seafood you can find, some cooked, some raw. At FishWorks, the *fruits de mer* has become a cult thing, and I offer the choice of raw mussels or cooked mussels, of raw clams or cooked. The initial reaction is to say 'cooked', but once people are persuaded to eat bivalves '*au naturel*', just like oysters, they are converted. They taste just like the sea. Some people like their scallops raw, but I have to say that unless they are the small queens, I prefer them cooked and don't include them as part of a *fruits de mer*. You can be flexible, but keep it strictly to shellfish. The only accompaniments needed are mayonnaise, all-i-oli, shallot vinegar (which is just good red wine vinegar with chopped shallots in), Tabasco both hot and mild, plenty of cut lemons and my shellfish sauce.

You will need shellfish crackers, shellfish picks and oyster forks, a plate and a shellfish stand. If you don't have any of these, a small hammer and some hatpins, nutcrackers and small forks will do fine, with the *fruits de mer* in a big salad bowl, piled on a few books in the middle of the table. As you make it more often, which I am sure you will during the summer, it is worth buying the proper kit, which will also come in useful for the occasional crab. You'll need to provide a large bowl for the debris.

Over the page there is a picture that shows some of the best things to include in a *fruits de mer*. Get a good gang of people together, with some great bottles of Muscadet or a good crisp dry white of your choice, and you will be in for a great time. Be adventurous, pile it high, enjoy the magnificent occasion. I don't need to tell you how good it will be – it will speak for itself.

Side Dishes: What Goes with What

Side dishes are a big part of my meals at home. At FishWorks the fish is cooked simply and you choose from a few fresh side dishes – it's a nice way to eat. You can introduce other flavours to your meal without taking anything away from the main star. A plate that is too fussy puts me off, while a simply cooked and dressed piece of fish and a big bowlful or two of something else on the table works for me. I serve side dishes in my favourite big white bowls, and every mealtime looks like a feast. You can use the same big bowl for two, four, six or eight people – just throw in the ingredients and drizzle over the dressing or oil.

Keep your side dishes simple. The first of the Jersey Royals, simply buttered with mint, fresh runner beans just boiled and finished in butter – produce as good as this stands up for itself. If your greengrocer has some fresh crisp sensational lettuces, the choice is made for you, you don't even have to think.

Even with side dishes my golden rule is good produce. Without it, reach for the tin opener!

Braised Fennel with Chilli, Lemon and Thyme

This is good with any piece of fish. I think fennel was meant to be eaten with seafood. It can be eaten hot or cold, and you can serve it as a side dish or add a few mussels and clams and serve it as a main course.

You will need (serves 4) 4 small fennel bulbs (if you can get baby ones these are best, and allow 2 per person) — 200 ml dry white wine — 2–3 sprigs of fresh thyme — 2 cloves of garlic, peeled and sliced — 1 teaspoon coriander seeds and 1 teaspoon fennel seeds, toasted (to toast them, put them into a small dry frying pan and heat until they start to smell fragrant) — ½ a mild red chilli, finely chopped — juice of 1 lemon — ½ a wineglass of Pernod — 50 ml good olive oil — salt and freshly ground black pepper — a handful of fresh parsley, chopped

To make Preheat the oven to 180°C/350°F/gas 4. Put all the ingredients except the parsley into a casserole dish with a tight-fitting lid. Bring to a simmer and bake in the preheated oven for 30–40 minutes or until the vegetables are soft and tender. Remove from the oven, check the seasoning, add the parsley and serve at room temperature or chilled.

Grilled Onions with Halloumi, Walnuts and Mint

This is a wonderful summery side dish and is perfect with red mullet and sardines. If you are cooking for vegetarians it makes a great starter. The walnut and mint dressing is worth making in quantity as it is useful for dressing fish like sea bass, bream and hake. Halloumi is a Cypriot sheep's milk cheese which keeps for ever in your fridge and is wonderfully salty. It is good grilled – try it with the grilled Italian onions that are available in jars at many supermarkets. Add some fresh mint and toss everything together for another easy and delicious side dish.

You will need (serves 4) 1 onion, sliced into rings — 100 ml olive oil — salt and freshly ground black pepper — 4 slices of halloumi cheese — 4 walnuts — a handful of fresh mint — juice of ½ a lemon

To make Brush the onions with oil and season with salt. Cook on a grill plate until nicely charred but still crunchy on each side. Put some on each serving plate, with a slice of halloumi on top. Blitz the walnuts, mint, olive oil and lemon juice in a food processor and drizzle liberally over the top with a good twist of black pepper.

Peas with Prosciutto and Parsley

You can make a few handfuls of frozen peas taste delicious with some black pepper and crisp prosciutto. This is how you do it.

You will need (serves 4) olive oil — 4 slices of prosciutto, very finely shredded — 4 handfuls of frozen peas, thawed — a knob of butter — freshly ground black pepper — a handful of fresh parsley, chopped — optional: lemon juice

To make Heat the olive oil in a pan large enough to take the peas, and fry the prosciutto until just crisp. Add the peas and a knob of butter and season with black pepper. Stir until the peas are just warmed through, then add the parsley. Season with lemon juice if you wish.

10-DAYS SPECIAL

HALIBUT / SQUID
TURBOT / RINGS

SKATE COLEY

FRESH HADDOCK

COD FILLETS

PLAICE

Roasted Broccoli with Anchovy, Garlic and Chilli

I like to roast vegetables, and broccoli is no exception. There is so much flavour in the stalk, which people often throw away. Just peel its tough outer skin and cook it with the florets. This anchovy sauce is quite pungent. You can make it in large quantities – it stores well in the fridge and is good for warming through and dipping raw vegetables, like carrots or celery, into for a quick starter. It is also a good standby for spooning over a grilled tuna steak.

You will need (serves 4) 2 medium-sized heads of broccoli — 100 ml good olive oil — 25 g butter — 1 clove of garlic, finely chopped — 1 tin of salted anchovy fillets (drain off the oil) — 1 tiny dried red chilli

To make Preheat the oven to 200°C/400°F/gas 6. Peel the stem of the broccoli, then cut each head into 4 or 6 lengthways, leaving the florets intact. Place on a roasting tray, drizzle with a little olive oil and sprinkle with a little water, and roast in the preheated oven for 10 minutes. Place a glass bowl over a steaming pan of water. Add the butter and let it melt – when it is just starting to foam, add the garlic and the anchovies and continue to stir. Do not let the butter brown. Stir until all the anchovies have melted, then pour in the olive oil and crumble in the chilli. This sauce is quite pungent. If it is too strong for you, simply melt some butter and stir a teaspoonful into the sauce before dressing the broccoli.

Try roasting chunks of marrow, red onions, peppers and aubergines, either together or individually, and serving them with this sauce.

Roasted Pepper, Dried Tomato, Barley and Basil Salad

This is a nice refreshing simple salad that is good with almost anything. Serve it in a bowl for everyone to help themselves. Grill a few prawns and toss them in, still in their shells, for a simple starter.

You will need (serves 2) 1 roasted red pepper, peeled and diced — 2–3 sun-dried tomatoes, very finely shredded — 100 g cooked barley — juice of 1 lemon — olive oil — a handful of fresh basil, chopped — a small handful of fresh parsley, chopped — a pinch of salt — freshly ground black pepper

To make Mix everything together. Taste and season with salt and freshly ground black pepper. If more moisture is needed, add more olive oil and lemon juice. The flavours should be fresh, clean and summery and the barley soft and chewy to the bite.

Roasted Tomatoes with Green Olive Tapenade

These roasted tomatoes have never been off the menu at FishWorks. They have been served dressed with pesto, with anchovies, in fact with just about anything, and they are always popular. I always have them in my kitchen and they end up in pasta sauces, in braised beans, on my plate for breakfast with grilled sausages and bacon with a sprinkling of Worcestershire Sauce. They are also good rubbed on to fresh chunks of bread before dunking into all-i-oli.

You will need (serves 2) 6 roasted tomato halves (see page 44) — a small handful of green pitted olives — 1 clove of garlic — 3 anchovy fillets — 50 ml olive oil — optional: fresh basil leaves

To make Put all the ingredients except the tomatoes into a food processor and blitz to a smooth paste. Put the tomatoes on a plate and dress with this mixture. Finish with a few torn basil leaves if you like.

Broad Bean Salad with Mahón Cheese and Sweet Peppers

This is a salad I made up while shopping at the town market in Mahón on the island of Menorca. Everything looked so good, but I settled on broad beans and peppers. Mahón is famous for cheese-making, but you don't see much of it in the UK. It's a pity, because the cheese is delicious: the young ones are soft and mild and the aged ones are hard and crumbly. Parmesan would be a good substitute.

You will need (serves 4) 1 tablespoon vinegar — a glug of olive oil — sea salt — 4 handfuls of broad beans, blanched and peeled — 2 red peppers, roasted, peeled and deseeded (see note below) — 1 tablespoon fresh oregano leaves — a few shavings of Mahón cheese (I prefer the mild variety)

To make Mix together the vinegar, olive oil and a pinch of sea salt in the bottom of a large bowl. Add the broad beans, roasted peppers and oregano and toss together until well coated. Spoon on to a serving plate and top with shavings of the cheese.

A note on roasting peppers I find the best way to do this is to blacken them on a barbecue or on a roasting tray in the oven for 15–20 minutes. When they are done, put them into a plastic bag and twist the top to seal it. Leave until they are cool enough to handle. There will be lots of juice at the bottom of the bag, which is worth saving and whisking with the dressing. Take them out of the bag, peel off the skin and scrape off the seeds.

Cucumber and Onion Salad
with Dill

Try this with anything grilled.

You will need 1 teaspoon caster sugar — 100 ml white wine vinegar — 1 cucumber, seeds removed, chopped into small chunks — ½ a red onion, finely diced — 4 spring onions, finely sliced — a handful of fresh dill, chopped — salt and freshly ground black pepper

---

To make Dissolve the sugar in the vinegar, then stir in the cucumber, onion, spring onions and dill. Chill for 30 minutes and season with salt and freshly ground black pepper before serving.

Lime, Cucumber and Mint Salad

Nice and simple, clean and refreshing.

You will need (serves 4) 1 cucumber, cut in half lengthways — 1 teaspoon caster sugar — juice of 2 limes — a glug of olive oil — a handful of fresh mint, chopped — salt and freshly ground black pepper

---

To make Scoop the seeds from the cucumber with a dessertspoon and discard. Slice the cucumber into little half-moons. Dissolve the sugar in the lime juice and whisk in a glug of olive oil and plenty of mint. Season the cucumber with a little salt and freshly ground black pepper, then spoon the dressing over the top and toss together.

Newlyn Brill

Pan-fry and serve with black butter, capers and clams.

£18.59

FISH
WORKS

Olive, Romaine Lettuce, Bread and Cheese Salad

This is a good salad which you can throw together with ingredients that are often knocking about in the kitchen.

You will need (serves 4) 1 romaine or cos lettuce — a good handful of mixed green and black olives (the ones marinated in garlic and herbs are best) — a handful of fresh basil leaves, roughly torn — 1 small mozzarella cheese — lemon juice or lemon oil — a chunk of stale bread — 100 ml best-quality olive oil — some parmesan cheese shavings

To make Put the lettuce leaves into a large bowl. Sprinkle with the olives and basil, then tear the mozzarella over the top and drizzle with the lemon juice or lemon oil. Tear the bread into bite-sized chunks and soak in your best olive oil. Sprinkle these on top and finish with the parmesan shavings.

Grilled Courgette Salad with Mint Leaf and Garlic

You don't have to limit this to courgettes; peppers, aubergines, sliced onions – anything Mediterranean will work well. When I am cooking these at home I use a hot grill or frying pan, but you'll get the best flavour from cooking over a wood fire or barbecue.

You will need (serves 4) 4 courgettes, sliced thinly lengthways (I use my mandolin to slice them a little thicker than a good crisp) — good olive oil — sea salt — 1 clove of garlic, finely chopped — a handful of fresh mint, chopped — 3–4 tablespoons sherry vinegar

To make Toss the sliced courgettes in a little olive oil, salt and half the garlic. Grill for 2–3 minutes either side on the grill plate or barbecue. Arrange on a serving plate, sprinkle with the remaining chopped garlic, the mint, sherry vinegar and plenty of your favourite olive oil. They are best served at room temperature after allowing the flavours to develop for an hour or so.

Some Great Markets
and Restaurants

Every European city is served by a good wholesale food market. Next time you take a city break, do something different and include the market in your visit. You won't regret it.

To be able to cook well we all need inspiration, something that sparks us off and gets us excited. A quick conversation, a recommendation or a paragraph in a book can do that. Most of the recipes in this book have been influenced by conversations with taxi drivers, chefs, fishermen and fellow drinkers in a busy early morning market bar. I can remember how I got hold of, or created, each recipe and where and with whom I first ate it.

I would place a good night out at a market as one of my favourite things to do. I have been to some fabulous ones just a cheap air fare away in Barcelona and Paris, and some others further afield, in Sydney and Singapore. Street markets are one thing, but wholesale markets are another. They are so big, you will be amazed. They have their own road systems! They all have bars and restaurants which are open all night for the market workers. Don't plan on buying anything, though, as many merchants won't be allowed to sell direct to you. This visit is purely for fun. It really will be worth the effort if food is your thing.

I like eating out – it's great fun and entertainment. You learn so much, and often you don't even realize it at the time. Sometimes, though, you eat or see something and immediately you just want to cook it or share it. Eating out, or in, with friends and family and talking about food is an essential part of being a good cook. My food and cooking education has been at the hands of others. I'm grateful to those many people because they have added so much enjoyment to my life. The restaurants listed on the following pages are ones I think are outstanding. None of them are posh or chef-led (not that there is anything wrong with that), they just serve some of the best fish I have eaten in simple surroundings.

Wholesale Fish Markets

Mercabarna, Barcelona

Director's name: Daniel Martinez Menchón (a really helpful chap)
Address: Centre Directiu, 5a Planta Zona Franca, Sector C, 08040 Barcelona
Tel: 93.335.53.00
e-mail: mb@mercabarna.es
Website: www.mercabarna.es

Make sure when you go to this market that you are in good company. I dragged my friend Roy Morris out of a restaurant and then his hotel room to take him here. I am not sure he knew what to expect, but I know that he now cherishes it as one of the best evenings he's ever spent, so much so that it tempted him after ten years of being a vegetarian to try a little pata negra and even to walk around the meat part of the market. This market is huge: the fish section is over 4,500,000 square feet, has fifty-two fish merchants trading in it and sells over 100,000 tonnes of fish per year. I came eye to eye with tuna and swordfish as big as myself, sardines so small I didn't think they should have been there, mountains of octopus, sea urchins and clams. Expect to find shellfish like percebes, or goose barnacles as they are known, and an array of other things from around the Spanish coast that you won't have come across in the UK. (You can also see a lot of boxes labelled 'Origin: Cornwall, England', which says a lot about the quality of our fish.)

If you can't make it to the Mercabarna go to the Boquería, which is a retail food market on the Ramblas. There are fish stalls, butchers, greengrocers, delicatessens, bars and restaurants. It is a fab place with a great atmosphere.

Rungis, Paris

Address: Espace Rungis, Marché International de Rungis, 1 Rue de la Tour, 94152 Rungis
Tel: 01 41 80 81 22
e-mail: webmaster@semmaris.fr
Website: www.rungisinternational.com

Rungis is situated about twenty minutes south of the périphérique from Paris. It is a huge market. It deals in fish, meat, cheese, vegetables, anything you can possibly imagine. It is a trading point for produce from the rest of Europe and the world. It has its own system of roads, the size of motorways, and lorries thunder in and out throughout the night bringing fresh produce and taking away food that has already been sold to other destinations around the world. You need a pass to get in, and you certainly won't be able to buy anything, but there are twenty-five restaurants and bars in the market and you can almost get lost in those for a few days!

Rungis also organize tours which you can book via their website, in advance of your trip. The experience is definitely not to be missed.

Sydney Fish Market, Australia

Address: Sydney Fish Market, Bank Street, Pyrmont, Sydney, New South Wales 2009
Tel: +61.2.9004.1122
e-mail: fishline@sydneyfishmarket.com.au
Website: www.sydneyfishmarket.com.au
Hours: Mon – Fri from 7.00 a.m.

Sydney fish market is the biggest of its kind in the southern hemisphere. It is not just the 2,500 crates of fish that it sells every day and the 100 species that it deals in, it is the retail area which is so enjoyable: sushi, fruit and vegetables, delicatessen, fishing tackle, fishmonger upon fishmonger and restaurant upon restaurant. It really is a vibrant, cutting-edge place. It offers tours of the commercial market, it has a cookery school, in fact it has everything you need to be able to enjoy good seafood. The management at the market are proud of it, and if you speak to them they are only too happy to help with any request you may have. It is a long way to go, but if you are ever out there, add it to your list of 'musts'.

Billingsgate Fish Market, London

Address: Billingsgate Market, Trafalgar Way, London E14 5ST
Tel: +44 (020) 7 987 1118
e-mail: iris.hindley@billingsgate-market.org.uk
Website: www.billingsgate-market.org.uk
Hours: Tues. – Sat. 5.00 a.m. – 8.30 a.m.,
Sun. (shellfish market) – 6.00 a.m. – 8.00 a.m., Mon. – Closed

Billingsgate is definitely worth a trip. It is an open market, which means that you can buy fish directly from the merchants. They won't, however, prepare it for you and you will have to get up early. It is worth getting there at about two or three in the morning, having a coffee and breakfast in the café watching the fish arrive and listening to the characters around you. You won't be able to buy until five o'clock when the bell is rung, though. There are over fifty merchants, some of which have been there since Billingsgate first opened. One of the merchants I can recommend is Simon Newnes, whose company is called C.J. Newnes and Partner. Simon and his partner Brian import and sell some magnificent fish, not only from our coast but from the Spanish and French markets too. J. Bennett is another good merchant, as is Ray Young – both deal in exotic species from the rest of the world. If you are going to buy from the market, make sure you read pages 7-11 first.

Newlyn Fish Auctions

Newlyn Harbour, Cornwall
They operate from Monday to Saturday.

This is where it all starts, once the fish has been landed. I find the fish auctions at Newlyn fascinating. On a good day the market is trading in over thirty species, fish for the domestic and export market. You won't be able to buy here, but it is good just to be around. The times of the auction vary from day to day dependent on weather and landings, but getting there at between 7.30 and 8 a.m. usually gets you a viewing. (Don't make the journey, however, if there are very strong winds.) Rob Wing, our fish buyer and supplier to Fish-Works, has been buying and working off the market for over twenty years. Rob is a great friend and he has shown me how the market works and taken me there many a time to learn the art of wholesale fish buying – but I am no closer to cracking it. You will see what I mean when you get there. The auctioneer speaks so quickly and it is difficult to know what is going on, but nevertheless it is a great experience.

Restaurant Listings

FishWorks Bath

6 Green Street, Bath
Tel: 01225 448707

FishWorks Bristol

128 Whiteladies Road, Bristol
Tel: 0117 974 4433

FishWorks Chiswick

6 Turnham Green Terrace, Chiswick, London W4 1QP
Tel: 0208 994 0086

FishWorks Christchurch

10 Church Street, Christchurch, Dorset
Tel: 01202 487 000

Opening times: Tues. – Sat., 9 a.m. – 10.30 p.m.

The FishWorks restaurants are café style. They are informal places to eat, with all the emphasis being on fresh fish. The atmosphere is busy: customers are queuing at the fish counter and chatting to the chefs who work behind it, while diners are drinking, cracking crabs and lobsters and enjoying simply cooked fish from the menu and the daily specials which are created from the day's landings. The quality of the fish is second to none, and as well as being cooked in the kitchen it is sold daily from 9.00 in the morning until 10.30 in the evening. Wines are available for retail too. If you can't get to the FishWorks counter to buy fish to cook at home there is a home delivery, next-day service. You will receive the same fish direct from the coast that is sold and cooked in the restaurants. I regularly enjoy fabulous meals at the restaurants and have never been anywhere else where the fish is so consistently fresh. For further information about any of the individual sites see the Which? *Good Food Guide*.

Trattoria al Gatto Nero da Ruggero

Via Giudecca 88, 30012 Burano, Venezia

Tel: 041 730 120

One of the most fabulous restaurants I have ever been to. It is simple and typically Venetian. The owner's son, Max, speaks perfect English and is passionate about his food and wine. He will ensure that you have the very best of what the lagoon and the Adriatic have to offer. I would place the simply fried sea bass among other things that Penny, Isobel and I had there as one of the best things I have ever eaten. Well worth a visit.

Hostaria da Franz

Venezia – Castello, Fond, S. Giuseppe, 754, (Zona Giardini Biennale)

Tel: 041 522 0861

www.hostariadafranz.com

A long-established restaurant run by a wonderful Austrian chef called Franz. Franz has had the restaurant for fourteen years and it is popular with the Venetians. His food is simple with a modern touch and his grilled eel is the best I have ever eaten.

Restaurante S'Espigo

Moll de Llevant, 267 Port de Mao, 07701 Mahón, Menorca

Tel: 971 36 99 09

My favourite restaurant in the whole world, so far. The owners, Anna and Juan, still cook and run the restaurant after seventeen years and there is no sign that they will ever give up. The seafood is magnificent and changes daily. It depends on what is brought in to the restaurant, often while you are sitting down having a meal. The tables outside need to be booked and people tend to eat late, so the restaurant is buzzing until the early hours of the morning and every last piece of fish is gone. They always have a leg of pata negra ham, which is carved by hand to order. You have to try it.

Rui, Restaurante Marisqueira

R. Comendador Vilarinho 27, Silves, Portugal
Tel: 28 244 2682

When someone recommended a fish restaurant 40 kilometres from the coast I was a little surprised, but decided to give it a try and walked through a door off a back street in the town into a room stacked with vivier tanks which contained all sorts of shellfish, from clams to lobsters and crabs. I ate a fantastic seafood cataplana which was nothing but traditional. I had some pork with clams, and for the first time I tried goose barnacles, which are strange to look at but outstanding to eat. This was every bit my kind of fish restaurant. A bit FishWorks style.

Acknowledgements

Massive thanks to Roy Morris for the heaps of support and encouragement – you've been a real star. Mathew Prowse (the Clam), who spent so much time in the kitchen with me – cheers, mate. My fantastic agent, Dinah Wiener. Pete Cassidy and Kate Whitaker, I've been lucky to work with you, the photos are ace. My editor, Annie Lee. All at Michael Joseph, especially Lindsey Jordan for her belief in this book from the start and for giving me a shot; John Hamilton for the art direction and the great fun we had throughout – thanks, mate. Robert Clifford-Wing for his support and enthusiasm; Chandos Elletson – great inspiration; Laura Cowan – big big thanks; John Croft, Derry Treanor, Roger Murray-Leach, thanks for your ongoing belief. Cloggs, Gazza, Dave, Jacko and Nick, who readily did anything that was needed to help. Mum, Dad, Carly – big thanks always, for everything. Ad, Mikey, Tets and the gang – thanks, dudes. A special thanks to Karen, Jen, Choc and all the guys at FishWorks who believe in it all as much as I do. Fran and Blue for being great tasters. My beautiful daughters, Sadie and Isobel, and my son, Ben, heaps of love – you're fantastic. Pen, thanks for giving me the freedom to do it all.

Index

Page numbers in **bold** denote illustration

roasted cod with fennel, mustard, ginger and
chicory salad 94, **95**
feta cheese
parsley, mint, walnut and feta pesto 22
fish
fingers and mayonnaise 100
stew (zarzuela) 131
white fish and broad bean risotto with saffron
and parsley 85
fried herring roes on toast with anchovy, rosemary
and gherkins 63
fried swordfish Milanese style with wild oregano and
anchovy 42, **43**
fritto misto **118**, 119
fruits de mer 171

G

garlic
all-i-oli 25
baked sea bass with roasted whole garlic,
rosemary and chilli 136, **137**
baked shellfish with bucatini, whole roasted
garlic and thyme 50, **51**
butter 28
grilled mussels stuffed with pancetta, garlic and
green pepper 105
grilled queen scallops with anchovy, roasted
garlic and mint 108
hake with crisp sweet garlic and good olive oil
90, 91
pan-roasted sea bass with sea salt, garlic and
rosemary 140, **141**
parsley, garlic, hazelnut and salted anchovy
pesto 22–3
razor clams with parsley, garlic and hazelnuts
132, **133**
roasted broccoli with anchovy, garlic and chilli
182
sautéd spider crab with garlic, lemon and parsley
48, **49**
gazpacho with seafood 154
gherkins
fried herring roes on toast with anchovy,
rosemary and 63
ginger
bream ceviche with chilli, coconut and 152, **153**
and lime marinade 32

roasted cod with fennel, mustard, ginger and
chicory salad 94, **95**
roasted langoustines with ginger, chilli and
coriander butter 164
gnocchi
cod steaks with potato gnocchi, chilli and rich
tomato sauce 120, **121**
gooseberry vinegar 35–6
green peppers
grilled mussels stuffed with pancetta, garlic and
105
grilled courgette salad with mint leaf and garlic 189
grilled cured anchovies with wild oregano 156,
157
grilled monkfish with rosemary and caprice salad
44, **45**
grilled mussels stuffed with pancetta, garlic and
green pepper 105
grilled onions with halloumi, walnuts and mint 180
grilled queen scallops with anchovy, roasted garlic
and mint 108
grilled salt cod with olive oil and wine vinegar 93
grilled sardine and tomato paste 99
grilled tuna with baked aubergines, tomato, cumin
and mozzarella 129
grilled tuna with oregano, oil, lemon and sea salt 47

H

haddock
with creamed leeks, runner beans and chervil
122, 123
see also smoked haddock
hake
braised hake with shellfish, parsley and peas
88
with crisp sweet garlic and good olive oil **90**,
91
halloumi
grilled onions with halloumi, walnuts and mint
180
ham
John Dory with cured ham, mozzarella, chilli and
basil leaf 146
hazelnuts
parsley, garlic, hazelnut and salted anchovy
pesto 22–3
razor clams with parsley, garlic and 132, **133**